YOU NEVER LEAVE BROOKLYN

EMANUEL CELLER

YOU
NEVER LEAVE
BROOKLYN

The Autobiography
of

EMANUEL CELLER

THE JOHN DAY COMPANY
NEW YORK

To Stella, Jane, Judy, and Sydney

Acknowledgement

To Bess Effrat Dick, who served under me as Chief of Staff of the House Committee on the Judiciary, I express my deepest appreciation and gratitude in the knowledge that without her indispensable aid and counsel this book could not have been written.

Foreword

You never leave Brooklyn. The life that spills over from Pitkin Avenue follows you to the placid, well-ordered Connecticut Avenue of Washington, D. C. The hoops, the kites, the skates, the sleds, the fights of Brooklyn's children follow you to the streets of official Washington, where no children scamper through the streets or tumble under your feet. The shadow of Brooklyn tenements falls upon the low houses of Washington.

Externally Washington is a lady—proper, hatted and gloved, as becomes a lady. Brooklyn is a woman, overlarge, aproned for work, with a crisscrossed heart.

Thirty years ago I came to Congress to represent what was then New York's Tenth Congressional District. In the thirty years I have talked to the great and the near great; to presidents and makers of presidents; to the Churchills and the Nehrus and the Orlandos of history. In thirty years you meet a lot of people. In thirty years you see a lot of causes a-borning and a-dying.

What I said, what I did, how I voted, what I thought, I realize now, as I look past the waves of the years, has been fashioned by Brooklyn. . . .

I have tried to set forth my thirty years in Congress because I feel that these years have a significance beyond the personal. Thirty years of unbroken participation in the national scene affords me, I believe, a perspective of our national history which may bear some value in future assessment. In the final analysis, however, this must—if it is to have any validity at all—be a personal evaluation. I have hastened, therefore, to make clear that this story is shaped as much by what I saw, felt, and heard in Brooklyn as it is by what I saw, felt, and did in Washington.

YOU NEVER LEAVE BROOKLYN

Chapter One

What now? What next? In the thirty years since 1923, when I first came to Congress, I have seen the years divide themselves almost visibly into four eras:

(1) The emotional and economic high fevers of the crowded twenties.

(2) The shock-struck years of the depression, when fear gripped the nation, fear from which it has never quite recovered. In this era I would include the changes in the concept of government, that is, the growing measure of governmental responsibility.

(3) The rise of totalitarianism and World War II.

(4) The East-West struggle.

I saw the swing of the pendulum from the war-breeding victory of isolationism to the uncertain, hesitant adoption of internationalism. When I came to Congress, a giant seemed to be awakening beneath the

3

crust of the earth. He was beginning to heave in restlessness. But as yet the surface was smooth.

The fight against joining the League of Nations had, as a matter of fact, already been won in 1923. We were self-sufficient, we were rich, we were throwing off the shackles of Europe in our literary and art forms. We, in Congress, did not worry. Harding was President. Congress was passing such legislation as the Northern Pacific Halibut Act, for protection of halibut fisheries; establishing the probation system in United States courts; authorizing the conservation, production and exploitation of helium gas; establishing the Library of Congress Trust Fund Board.

But here I must pause. The 68th Congress also passed the Immigration Act of 1924.

This was my first big lesson, with many little lessons thrown in for good measure. It was the same lesson I was to learn over and over again. The enactment of law is seldom, if ever, a careful structure built on bricks of logic.

The passage of the Immigration Act of 1924 resulted from a mixture of passion and emotion; a mixture of fears and hates, tempered by idealism and by vision, which lie behind the complex motivations of Congressional action. We were afraid of foreigners; we distrusted them; we didn't like them.

Under this act only some one hundred and fifty odd thousands would be permitted to enter the United

4

States. If you were of Anglo-Saxon origin, you could have over two-thirds of the quota numbers allotted to your people. If you were Japanese, you could not come in at all. That, of course, had been true of the Chinese since 1880. If you were southern- or eastern-European, you could dribble in and remain on sufferance.

In the twenties—the years of the high prices and the low waistlines—the United States was drawing her skirts about her in fear lest she be contaminated by the alien. The temper of the Congress, I discovered, *is* the temper of the country. To say that a handful of bitter men thwarted our entrance into the League of Nations is false. To say that a handful of men forced through the Immigration Act of 1924 is false.

The peace of the twenties was an uneasy peace because the people of the United States were erasing the memory of the war. The distrust of the League of Nations made no more sense to me than did the distrust of the aliens enacted into the Immigration Law.

I came from a district of aliens. I knew them. I knew the Irish and the Jews and the Italians and the Greeks. But in the debate in Congress—and so it has always been—what one talked about were issues, abstracts, masses; never people, never individuals. You didn't see people with brown eyes or bad teeth or big feet or curly hair. You talked of "the people," the "common man," or "private enterprise." There is always the basket phrase.

The Ku Klux Klan was gaining strength throughout the North and the South. The 18th Amendment was in effect. Prohibition was breeding gang wars and corruption in high places in Government. These were the sores now so apparent.

The surface calm of Congress never broke in the twenties. The troubled question of the tug of war between Germany and France, the bitter inflation in Germany, the wide, unchecked credit and corporate mergers in the United States, the fever of our own people to make merry, were off-stage fires we didn't care (or dare?) to see.

There were men older than I in Congress, men of more experience, of more learning. Yet the talk of the strength of America, her self-sufficiency, the profits and the prices did not fit into the picture I knew. I knew the women in the Brooklyn tenements who scrubbed their floors again and again in the helpless fight against squalor. I knew the timid, perplexed son of the immigrant—part of him Old World, part of him New—serious and hungry, filling the free schools and the free colleges of New York. I knew the Negro, kept down in poverty and degradation. The folklore of Poland, of Lithuania, of Russia, of Italy, became part of my folklore because I had heard it so often. I knew their richness and their laughter and the disappoint-

6

ing heartbreak of the struggle in America to adjust. I knew, also, their pride, the unfulfilled dream of independence that had first brought them here.

I would return from Washington each week end to my Brooklyn home on MacDonough Street—puzzled, tired, frustrated. A freshman congressman is a lost soul. He cannot find his way, literally and metaphorically. He has to learn his way about on the floor of the House and in committee. He doesn't know the rules and nobody bothers explaining them. Only back home among his friends and his visitors is he flattered by the sound of "Mr. Congressman." (I often wonder how difficult the path of a freshman congressman is these days, with the mushrooming growth of the alphabetical agencies and the complexity of the legislation before him.)

In my first two years of Congress I was not a happy man. I didn't like Washington climate; I didn't like Washington ideas. I was intolerant, impatient, and lost. I seemed to be climbing a greased pole. I was also ambitious. The years between 1923 and 1929 were plodding years. Coolidge replaced Harding and Hoover replaced Coolidge. These were the years of normalcy and mediocrity. Congress continued to enact such legislation as establishing the National Arboretum, the collection and publication of cotton statistics, extending the Animal Quarantine Act to live poultry, fixing standards for fruit and vegetable baskets.

For my part, I introduced and continued to introduce bills to amend the national prohibition act, for the relief and succor of starving populations in Germany, for providing for immigration commissions, to create a Negro industrial commission, and to provide for the investigation of labor conditions affecting employees rendering domestic service on railroads.

Then the rains came. The dams broke. And from that moment on we tumbled from crisis to crisis, dilemma to dilemma. In all the years to follow thereafter, the extraordinary was to become the commonplace, and we were all shockproof.

Congress began to skip, first in this direction, then in that. There were no leaders. Congress had not yet begun to feel the measure of its responsibility and the tragedies that arose from the 1929 crash. There was no plan; there was no direction. We were being thrust upward—all of us—into maturity, but we rebelled against the growth.

Congress, true, in early 1930 began to act piecemeal. Authorization for more public buildings was passed; authorization for greater road construction. There was no comprehension, none at all, of the relationship of our disaster to world disaster. The Smoot-Hawley Act (the Tariff Act of 1930 that was to strangle international trade) became law on June 23, 1930. The high protective tariff was conceived as a wall against further economic collapse.

The patchwork continued. The Reconstruction Finance Corporation was created. The Congress author-ized distribution of Government-owned wheat through the American National Red Cross for the relief of needy people of the United States. The Federal Home Loan Banks were established. Congress was in a fury of activity. It abolished lame duck Congresses; it provided for the independence of the Philippine Islands; it repealed the Eighteenth Amendment. At least it had risen from its deep sleep. It had opened one eye and begun to look, not only at its own country, but at the shadows that had also fallen over Europe.

As they had done to others, so did the tragedies long before forecast, shake me from my lethargy.

Chapter Two

. . . So, first of all, let me assert my firm belief that the only thing we have to fear is fear itself—nameless, unreasoning, unjustified terror which paralyzes needed efforts to convert retreat into advance.
—Franklin Delano Roosevelt:
Inaugural Address, March 4, 1933

The first days of the Roosevelt Administration charged the air with the snap and the zigzag of electricity. I felt it. We all felt it. It seemed as if you could hold out your hand and close it over the piece of excitement you had ripped away. It was the return of hope. The mind was elastic and capable of crowding idea into idea. New faces came to Washington—young faces of bright lads who could talk. It was contagious. We started to talk in the cloak rooms; we started to talk in committees. The shining new faces called on us and talked.

In March of 1933 we had witnessed a revolution—a revolution in manner, in mores, in the definition of

11

government. What before had been black or white sprang alive with color. The messages to Congress, the legislation; even the reports on the legislation took on the briskness of authority. I have asked myself often, "Did one man do this? If one did this, what manner of man was he?" I don't know. I think nobody does. Since those days I have read every bit of writing on Roosevelt: Perkins, Sherwood, Churchill, Eleanor Roosevelt, Flynn, Gunther. Out of these cascades of words no definite or sharp outline arises. Whenever I visited Roosevelt on official business, I found a man adroit, voluble, assured, and smiling. I was never quite sure he was interested in the purpose of my visit; we spent so little time on it.

Mostly he talked. He talked with seeming frankness, and when I left, I found that he had committed himself to no point of view. At the end of each visit I realized that I had been hypnotized. His humor was broad, his manner friendly without condescension. Of wit there was little; of philosophy, none. What did he possess? Intuition, yes. Inspiration, yes. Love of adventure, the curiosity of the experimental. None of these give the answer. None of these give the key. I believe his magic lay in one facet of his personality. He could say and he did say, "Let's try it." He knew how to take the risk. No other man in public life I knew could so readily take the challenge of the new. It was boldness without carelessness. He was neither self-questioning

12

nor afraid. I have seen a little bit of that in the man Ben-Gurion, Prime Minister of the little Republic of Israel. Yet, in Ben-Gurion there is a measure of caution, an inhibiting sensitivity arising from his vast store of ancient knowledge.

I have talked to those who have been inspired by Gandhi, for example. Their inspiration is tinged with awe, perhaps with mysticism. The adoration of Roosevelt was earthy, palpable. It could be mixed with good food, laughter, cold showers, an off-color joke. Yet it was not the same kind of heartiness you could ascribe to Churchill. Churchill was hearty, but of the grand manner. There is something of the symbol in Churchill. One didn't think of Roosevelt as a symbol. He was as personal as the morning coffee, so you felt.

It will be remembered prayerfully by many presidents to come that for almost four years after his taking office a comparative peace existed between President Roosevelt and the Congress. Inevitably, between the Congress and the President, whatsoever his name, the tug of war begins. How long the honeymoon lasts is anybody's guess. But with Roosevelt the times and the man coincided to permit the harmony to sustain itself for the longest period in our history. The new Congress in the face of the country's desperation could only follow where Roosevelt led. We needed the breath and the magic of Roosevelt and we fed upon him hungrily. But the usual self-assertion of the members of

Congress, with their individual traits, attitudes, and even passions, broke loose in 1937.

The first, the longest, and the loudest clamor against Roosevelt came with his plan for the reorganization of the Supreme Court. It shocked the Congress. I wonder now why the shock was so great. There was a consistency in Roosevelt's logic which we chose utterly to ignore. The "nine old men" on the bench were products of another age, tempered by social attitudes which the people had rejected in the bitterness of the depression. They had not swum in the swift rivers of the times and could not comprehend the currents. The Supreme Court could, by judicial interpretation, undo the work of the Congress and the President. Constitutional interpretation is just as much a matter of temperament as it is the knowledge of precedents. Yesterday's minority opinion becomes the majority opinion of today.

But we were shocked. I believe that we were looking for absolutes. The delicate constitutional balances must not be disturbed. In the rapid succession of legislative enactments, many of which were based on untried political theory, the Supreme Court, not subject to the short-ranging pressures of each day, was the brake against the impetuous, the experimental. In the Supreme Court lay certainty, assurance, and authority. These must not be disturbed.

Day after day in that month of February of 1937 members rose to attack. One member said:

> ... What the President suggests is tantamount to telling the Congress and the public that the judges of our highest tribunal who have reached the age of seventy are incompetent. But we know he does not really mean that; he cannot. What he does mean, but fails to say, is that they have not embraced the policy of New Dealism, that they have outlawed basic laws of the New Deal, and since he is hampered by the Constitution from involuntarily removing the old blood which is hostile to New Deal acts, he proposes to appoint to the court six new judges who will reflect the New Deal interpretation of the power of Congress under the Constitution and thus clear the way for the resurrection of the principles of the N. R. A., the A. A. A., and other proposals giving authority for Federal jurisdiction over social and economic problems of national scope, held unconstitutional by the Supreme Court. There can be little doubt that if the Congress accedes to the President's demand that we legislate into being a Court that would not rebuff his administration in the manner of a majority of the present Justices, the new members will be tacitly pledged to interpret the Constitution in the Rooseveltian

15

theory, namely, that the Federal Government has unlimited power over labor and property and the liberties of the people. The scheme evades the method of change provided in the Constitution. It is a device to make the Roosevelt will supreme. It is an effort to get hold of the Court and bend it to one man's will. It is merely a striking back at the Court's refusal to interpret contested passages of the Constitution unanimously his way.

Speeches like this were met by others as enthusiastic in defense as those in attack:

. . . They lay out a nice big playground, right in the heart of the Government, where the special-privilege boys may play football with the people's rights without fear of being disturbed by any law. The man in the street wants this condition remedied. He wants human rights protected as well as property rights. He wants the rights of the masses to be taken care of just the same as he wants the rights of collective wealth taken care of. If it is necessary to pack the Court to get our people back to work; to take them off the relief rolls and to give the farmer a chance to realize something from his labor; to save our children from the devastating influences of mills and factories; to remove the obstacles which the forces of reaction are throwing in the pathway of human progress, then in the name of the Constitution, then in the name of justice and in the name of humanity let us pack the Court, and let us pack it well. [Applause.]

I recall how, after an unusually impassioned speech I had made against the reorganization plan, President Roosevelt sent his emissary to me. Since I had been one of his staunchest admirers and supporters, the President asked me to reconsider my views. I refused. Could I not, then, be more temperate in my opposition? To this I could agree. For the *Congressional Record* of April 13, 1937 I stated:

"... Therefore, it is not the Constitution, but a debatable construction of the Constitution adopted by a bare majority of the Court, which has been blocking the New Deal program. I deplore the cunning manner in which some opponents of the President have been carrying on a Nation-wide campaign to obscure this fact; and to make the people believe that Congress and the President have been trying to exercise powers which were clearly unconstitutional. I say this despite the fact that I disagree with the President's plan for six young additional Judges to replace those eligible for retirement. I sympathize with the President's objective but disagree with his method of obtaining it.

17

"For four years all the reactionary forces in the United States have been trying to convince the people that adequate laws could not be enacted by the Congress to aid the farmers, the wage earners, and small-business men, because the Constitution prohibited all such laws. But the fact is that the Constitution grants ample power to the Congress to pass such needed legislation, according to the opinions of several Justices of the Supreme Court, and of many other judges and lawyers of high authority and reputation. In other words, I believe the majority of the Supreme Court was wrong and the minority right.

"When one group of lawyers and judges upholds the constitutionality of desirable laws and another group declares such laws to be unconstitutional it is perfectly plain that, in the language of Chief Justice Hughes, 'the Constitution is what the judges say it is.'

"The Constitution has not prevented New Deal legislation. It is the judges who interpret the Constitution to conform to their ideas of public policy, and who do not believe in the wisdom of the New Deal program, who have blocked that program. They have nullified legislation which other judges equally able and learned hold to be within the powers of Congress. But, I repeat, the President has, I believe, taken the wrong means to prevent future nullification of New Deal legislation.

"Asking for six new appointments, if six over seventy fail to resign, is a rather bitter pill for the nation to swallow. It sticks in the throat. . . ."

Today I would still oppose such a plan. Whether I would be so deeply shocked at its proposal is yet another question.

Least understandable today is how quickly the name of Roosevelt has faded from public and private conversation. It was to be expected that around the figure of Roosevelt a flock of myths and legends would grow and become imbedded in our folklore. This has not happened. You no longer hear, as you heard for six months after Roosevelt's death, "We shall miss him; we shall miss him sorely." There is no speculative query, "What would Roosevelt have done?" I remark upon it because I had fully expected—as did millions of others of our people, as did the people of Europe and Asia—that the haze of Roosevelt's personality would linger over the country for many, many years to come. Perhaps this is a natural phenomenon. Perhaps no such intensity of adulation can sustain itself after a man's death. Emotions have evaporated, even the emotions of those who, after Roosevelt's death, continued to speak of him with a personal hatred that transcended reason. Why this is I do not know. The emotional response to Roosevelt was not for Roosevelt the Commander-in-Chief, for Roosevelt the war leader, but rather it was for the Roosevelt who, for the people, stood before the tide of the depression and held it back. The war years have blurred the image. Perhaps if Roosevelt, triumphant, confident, and smiling, had stood before the people on VE Day and VJ Day, the image would have been refreshened. I do not know. Perhaps he will spring to full life again when historians in a later day relate the excitements of his era.

Historians will record how Congress moved. Like so many cannon shots following one upon the other, Congress adopted emergency measure after another. March 9, the Emergency Bank Act; March 31, the Reforestation Act, providing work for the unemployed; May 12, the Agricultural Adjustment Act; May 12, the Inflation Act; May 18, the Tennessee Valley Authority Act; May 27, the Securities Act; June 5, the Gold Clause Repeal Resolution; June 6, the National Employment System Act; June 13, the Home Owners Loan Act; June 16, the National Industrial Recovery Act; June 16, the Public Works Act; June 16, the Farm Credit Act; June 16, creation of the Federal Deposit Credit Corporation.

I voted as the other Members of Congress did in those days of honeymoon between the Executive and Legislative branches of the Government. There was this difference though: I was not voting to remedy the new and different onslaught of economic distress which seemed suddenly to have descended upon us. I had come from a little bit of a world where economic distress had, it seemed, always been a part of life.

What I had known, what I had seen in Brownsville, Pitkin Avenue, in the Bushwick section of Brooklyn, in the Park Places of Brooklyn, in the markets of Brooklyn, had now become the generalized commonplace experience. I had known people hungry, cold, homeless, afraid, insecure. I was not talking and voting about anything new. I represented a district that had never known leisure, had never known freedom from want and freedom from fear. But I had now made a discovery about myself.

For the first ten years of my life in Congress, I had been timid. I had been too timid to tell the truth as I saw it. In a way I had betrayed my trust. Yes, I had fought against the unjust restriction of immigration. I worked what seemed to me endlessly on the repeal of the Prohibition Amendment. I had advocated the establishment of a Negro industrial commission. I had gestured against the growth of monopoly power. I had introduced a few civil rights bills. But, actually, I had taken on the color of the climate around me and I had driven back all the emotion that rose from the Brooklyn streets, so that I could belong unobtrusively to the exclusive club of Congress.

The panic of the depression loosened my inhibitions against being different. For the first time in ten years I could be myself. I realized that there were some things I cared about passionately. One of them was independence for India; another, the establishment of the National Homeland for the Jews in Palestine; another was our immigration laws; and the fourth was economic freedom for the people of the United States as against the growth of monopoly power stifling that freedom.

These are not unrelated areas. These are all assertions of independence, and in some curious way were directly related to my own new-found independence from the conventions of Congress. And in the same curious way, the thread that held them all together led back to the house where I was born.

The thread led back to my grandfather who, in 1848, had fled from Germany to find political freedom in the United States. In our house we repeated the pattern of thousands of other homes. There were a few books and a lot of music. Our food and our furniture were no different from our neighbors'. While we ourselves were not poor, I had only to walk a few streets away to find the sounds and the smells of poverty. We were respectable and middle-class. But we were not very far from the Brooklyn dockyards. I didn't know then that I would never be able to leave the sounds and smells of these sights behind me, but I was fiercely conscious of one thing—of my ambition. Where it would take me and where I would go, I didn't know.

I read whatever I could put my hands to. I became the "scholar" of the family. I became, too, more than just a bit of a snob. The studied, unquestioning pace of my family irritated me. There were "things" to be done. Nobody asked me what I meant by "things." I couldn't have defined them if I had tried. "Things" had to do with the study of music (this was a family interest), the books I read, and the dreams of travel, and the glimpses of elegance I caught on Fifth Avenue. But "things" had also to do with the way people were hurt and how, because they were hurt, they were angry and quarreled and were jealous of one another.

When I met Madame Vijaya Lakshmi Pandit many years later, before independence had been granted to India and before she had been appointed Ambassador to the United States, I found myself remembering the impotent rage I had felt at the sight of people oppressed by the meanness of poverty. In this cosmopolitan little woman of charm and discernment I could sense that same kind of rage and defiance against the degradation of her people. When she asked me to introduce her to President Truman—contrary to the tradition which imposed that responsibility on the British Embassy in Washington—I knew it to be her deliberate act of defiance. It was a scarcely-heard note of independence. When I did introduce her to President

Truman, no one caught that gesture or understood that it spelled independence. In that one little act she bound together for me rage against subjugation and the courage to act against it.

It was that kind of compulsion that took me step by step away from the pattern of my family into college and into law school. I, in part, "worked my way through school." This was not considered particularly heroic; it was the usual thing to do in my neighborhood. I discovered, in the practical way, the economic facts of life. My father was a wine merchant and I worked with him. Later, when Benjamin Fairless, president of United States Steel, appeared before the Committee on the Judiciary (of which I was Chairman), and I listened to his complacent explanation of United States Steel control of over fifty-one per cent of our ore, I remembered the wine routes of my youth. I have a lot more to say on the growth of monopoly power.

Chapter Three

The child is father of the man.
—William Wordsworth

The facts of my life are simple enough. The *Congressional Directory* of the 82nd Congress states:

EMANUEL CELLER; born in Brooklyn, N. Y., May 6, 1888; attended the public schools; was graduated from the Boys' High School of Brooklyn, in 1906, from Columbia College, New York City, in 1910, and from the Columbia University Law School, New York City, in 1912; admitted to the bar and commenced practice in New York City, in 1912; elected as a Democrat to the Sixty-eighth Congress, November 7, 1922; reelected to each succeeding Congress; chairman of the House Committee on the Judiciary; married and has two daughters—Judith S., and Jane B., married to Sydney B. Wertheimer; home address is 9 Prospect Park West, Brooklyn, N. Y.; Washington address, the Mayflower.

I know, though, that in writing this chapter I will have to sift through the pain and triumphs of the memories and half-memories that have piled up in sixty-four years of life. For me this will be hard work.

It has not been a life of adventure as we understand the word "adventure." Rather, it has been a life of internal excitements. The coming to grips with ideas—not things; the search, not for new lands, strange lands, but rather the search of the continents of the mind. I am not sure I can convey these kinds of excitements. Those who have felt their blood quicken with the awakening of a new thought or the discovery of a new purpose in the day will know what I mean.

The earliest memories of my grandmother, grandfather, my mother, father, two sisters, my brother, and myself all flow together. In the frame house on Sumner Avenue and Floyd Street, in Brooklyn, where I was born—the third child of four children—I grew up, knowing first of all the story book romance of my grandmother and grandfather. My grandfather was Catholic; my grandmother, Jewish. I have heard the story of their meeting so many times that it has taken on the form of a ballad. Crossing over from Bavaria, as immigrants to the United States, they did not meet on board ship. Outside of New York Harbor, the ship started to sink. My grandmother jumped overboard. My grandfather followed, to save this girl he had never met. Save her he did.

26

And so they were married. The courtship was short and intense, he promising to accept Judaism in return for her hand in marriage. Nine children were born of that marriage. My mother, Josephine, was fourth from the eldest. Six were girls; three, boys. The girls all married men of the Jewish faith, and those of the boys who married, married Christian women. The two groups, so cleanly split down the middle, separated. And there the story for me ended. I never asked, nor was I told, what happened in the main to the Christian branch of the family. Not that questions were *verboten;* they were just not asked.

I wish to report a happy childhood. I could not make drama out of it if I tried. There was my father—hearty, of great affability, a joiner of this club and that, providing well for his family. My mother, however—small, round, blue-eyed, gray-haired at an early age—was the center of my life. I loved her. I know no other way to say it. Her shyness disappeared only when she talked to me. My mother worked hard in the house, although we did have a maid-of-all-work as far back as I can remember. Mother was of a saving disposition. But there was no task that she would not put aside and no money which she would not spend for "Mannie." And only for "Mannie." My brother Mortimer and my sisters Jessie and Lilly could never, whatever the reason may have been, draw from her the warmth I did. To only one other person did she give the same measure of devotion, and that was my father. For Mannie she cherished secret ambition. I was to be different, famous, educated. She transmitted this urgency to me. It seems to me that forever after I was to try to grow into the image she had fashioned for and of me.

My father, too, did his very best to spoil me, singling me out from his other children for special treatment. If he talked music in our family group (and music was always part of the household), it was really to me he spoke. He loved to make political speeches and would accept all invitations to address the Odd Fellows or the Masons or the Democratic Club, of which he was a member. When he talked politics, he talked to me. I can't remember the time when I started to work around his store, which was on the first floor of the house in which we lived. He tried to teach me what he knew of his business, which was the rectifying of liquors, their bottling, and their distribution.

They were both determined, each in his own way, to "make something" of me. To their determination was added the determination of my grand uncle, Sam Grabfelder. "Uncle Sam" we called him. Sam Grab-felder was—to use the most awesome of words—a millionaire. He was a distiller in Kentucky and originated many of the whiskey brand names now famous. His only formal education was that of the "gymnasium" in Germany—equivalent to our high school plus a year or so of college. While he had made money and while he had a wealth of knowledge of books and music and paintings, which he had acquired himself, he envied the graces of those with formal schooling. He, too, then transferred his ambition to me. What he couldn't be, he often said, he wanted me to be.

Uncle Sam was a kind man who, knowing so much, could forgive so much. Because he worked a great deal among the poor, he would tell me of the poor, of what the accident of birth meant to millions of people. As a founder of the Jewish National Hospital for Consumptives (now National Jewish Hospital) in Denver (to which he had donated literally millions), he knew the sick, and he told me about them. I have not forgotten.

I remember now how my wife-to-be and I, after I had graduated from law school, went to see him. Only he could answer the two questions before us: "Shall we get married now? Shall I begin the practice of law, or continue being the successful wine salesman I had become, working my way through law school?"

"Get married now," he said in answer to the first question. To the second question, he parried with his own: "What do you really want to be?"

"I want to be a lawyer," I said.

"Then be one and I will help you. I am not giving the money to you," he continued; "It will be a loan. This is how you will pay me back: Some day, when someone stands before you in need of help, you will help him as I will help you. In this way only will I consider the loan repaid."

I don't know, I can only hope, that I repaid that loan.

I didn't realize, of course, that there were three people carefully cultivating me, encouraging my ambition, sharpening my dissatisfactions with the *status quo*. How my brother and two sisters felt about this—shall we call it "coddling"—I never knew. I still don't. Whatever resentments they felt have never been spoken or acted out.

My father and my mother and Uncle Sam challenged me constantly to meet the demands their affection and their ambition for me placed upon me. I was a good boy, working hard, playing hard, studying hard. It may be that to some a happy youth is not reconcilable with ambition, restlessness, and eagerness. I can only say it was so.

Although I tried to emulate my father in his gregariousness, I never quite succeeded. I did not have many friends. Like my mother I was shy, but I hid that shyness. I hid it so well that I, myself, stopped recognizing it for what it was—and is. It has become a commonplace for me to hear people say, after meeting me, "But, Mr. Celler, you don't mind my saying that I had a very different picture of you." They would go on to explain that my statements in the press and on the floor of the House gave an impression of a man aggressive, bold, a hard-hitter and a hard fighter. Instead of that, they found a man genial, with a fund of jokes and card- paper- and match-tricks. I can understand how startling that contrast can be. The headlines read: "Celler Demands Probe of Newsprint Monopoly," "Celler Condemns Immigration Restrictions," "Celler Denounces Anti-Labor Activities." It was not difficult to gain the impression that I was a man always demanding, condemning, denouncing. Publicly I became an irate gentleman, full of righteousness and implacable convictions.

I went to Boys' High School—naturally. I say "naturally" because Boys' High School then, as now, was the high school of scholarships. Boys of Brooklyn today will tell you, "It's a hard school." It was highly competitive, with emphasis on disciplinary studies such as mathematics and the sciences. Athletics played a relatively small part. Boys who went to Boys' High School were earnest, so earnest that the boys of other high schools did not consider them "regular" or good sports. It followed, then, that the drive developed at home was forwarded by the climate of the school. Attendance at Boys' High School meant that you were "in transit"; that is, it was a step, almost inevitably, to college. That was the magic word—"college." The boys in the Boys' High School—an all-boys school, of course—were the poor, the near-poor, and the not-so-poor. Most of them were the sons of immigrants, and to them college meant breaking away from the sounds, the smells, the language that the Old World had transplanted into a corner of the New. College was a conveyance which would transfer them from the life of the laborer and the petty tradesman—the tailor, the shoemaker, the grocer—which had been their fathers' lot. The dominant theme of all the bull sessions was, "What will you be when you grow up?" Professionals, always. Lawyers, actors, doctors, teachers, writers. Here and there a businessman, but not quite so frequently. Behind most of the boys were parents who dreamed of greatness for their sons and went without so that their sons could be "college boys."

I was among the few who were reckoned among the rich, "real-American," because my parents had been born in the United States. My father had grown wealthy in his business. By that time we owned our own home on Sumner and Park Avenues. It consisted of two stories above my father's whiskey rectifying business. We occupied the two stories, renting out two of the rooms. (My mother could not see these rest empty.) Perhaps that is why the bitterness and cynicism which was so much a part of the make-up of so many of the Boys' High School students never became my way. If I were writing fiction, the story would go otherwise. But can I not question, if only plaintively, if "it is easier for a camel to go through the eye of a needle, than for a rich man to enter into the kingdom of God"?

If I am talking about my days at high school, I must talk also about Stella. I don't want to talk about her. Stella is my wife. I don't want to talk about her because I have a feeling that what I do say about her will not be believed. I first met Stella while I was attending Boys' High School. It seems that all my life I have known her—this slight girl with the dark curls, the gray-blue eyes, and the lovely, fragile face. Stella, precise and delicate, was as if I had willed her to be. From the day I met her she was my girl. I made no pretense about it. I used to meet her every day at the corner of her school—Girls' High School—and walked her home, carrying her books in the good old traditional way. I read poetry to her and talked of my ambitions. In my freshman year at college we began to talk of getting married some day. We were both being very practical. I said there were many years ahead of me before, to use a good old Brooklyn expression, "I became established." She agreed. Everybody knew she was "Mannie's girl." The school club accepted her as mascot. She was always there anyway. My mother and father, although grieved that one so young should have become attached to one girl, made no effort to separate us. Stella's mother never stopped trying until our marriage. I was jeopardizing Stella's chances. By that time my father, through misplaced confidence in investments and people, had lost his money. My Uncle Sam was helping to finance my schooling at Columbia College.

Soon after I entered college my father died. My mother survived him only by five months. So great had been the attachment between the two that, upon my father's death, my mother took to her bed and never left it. While my father was alive, the strength that he gave her enabled her to withstand the ravages of her own illness, but with his death, her courage evaporated.

I became head of the household. Following his financial collapse, my father had given up his business and had become a wine salesman. I took up his route. I went to school in the mornings and sold wines all afternoon until seven o'clock in the evening. I had my dinner and from seven to ten o'clock stayed with my mother, talking to her, comforting her and finally putting her to bed. My mother had consented to having a nurse only on the condition that I would spend the last part of each of her days with her. After ten o'clock I went to my studies and worked at them until two o'clock in the morning. It would seem then that I had had no time for study.

Stella could so easily have persuaded herself that I had pushed her out of my life. But Stella stayed. She was there when I started on the wine route, and she was there when I returned. Stella was with me when I took Italian lessons twice a week so that I would be better equipped to talk to the customers who were mostly of Italian origin.

Stella is always with me.

Chapter Four

Time's the king of men,
He's both their parent, and he is their
grave,
And gives them what he will, not what
they crave.
—Shakespeare: *Pericles. II*

It seems odd that throughout the six years of my attendance at Columbia, the thing I remember most is that I never had time. The same feeling oppresses me today—I never have time. As I write this, I am thinking of tomorrow. At ten-thirty I must appear before the Committee on Rules to urge the granting of a rule on a bill to increase the Federal judgeships. I keep reminding myself that I must review the crowded Federal dockets in each State of the Union and make a note of how far behind the district courts are in bringing cases to conclusion.

At the same hour—ten-thirty in the morning—I must appear before the Committee on House Administration to urge the granting of additional funds to enable the Committee on the Judiciary to carry forward its work. I must make a note to jot down how many hearings the Committee on the Judiciary has held, the number of hearings held by the Special Subcommittee to Investigate the Department of Justice. I don't want to forget to speak of the work of the Special Subcommittee on Reapportionment and the work of the subcommittee on Patents, Copyrights and Trade-marks. Add, I tell myself, the work of the Immigration Subcommittee which is currently studying the problem of expellees or refugees from Communist and Communist-dominated lands.

I keep thinking that tomorrow I must meet with other members of my special subcommittee to study the legislation before us which came as a result of the seizure by the President of the steel industry on April 8, 1952. I keep reminding myself that I must study the implications of the six-to-three decision of the Supreme Court in the case of *The Youngstown Sheet and Tube Co., et al* vs. *Charles Sawyer,* Secretary of Commerce.

I must remember to make a motion on the floor to appoint conferees to discuss the Senate disagreement with the House version of the bill to extend the President's emergency powers.

I must remind myself to read the report on the bill to increase the penalty for the theft or receipt of stolen mail matter generally.

I must remember to review the case for the increase

in payment to referees in bankruptcy, so that I can discuss this with a delegation which will be in my office at two o'clock in the afternoon.

I have just remembered my new assignment to a Select Committee to Conduct an Investigation and Study of Offensive and Undesirable Books, Magazines, and Comic Books. I must make another note to review the decision in the *Ulysses* case. I must remind myself to reread the testimony before the Kefauver Crime Committee on the effects on children of comic books. I disagree loudly with the setting up of such a censorship committee. That Congress is asked to set itself up as censor is carrying the duties of Congress to absurdity. Such an investigation has no point, except, perhaps, to educate the members of the committee in determining that the word "undesirable" is a nondefinable adjective when applied to the word "books." I feel strongly about this. I think it is an insult to human intelligence and intellectual freedom. Let us eliminate the home, parents, schools, and let Congress become the arbiter as to what every resident in the United States shall eat, drink, wear, read, and think!

But I haven't the time to examine all of this before me, I keep crying to myself. It seems that I am always being pushed by time to make decisions in blacks and whites.

In college and at law school it seemed it was the same way. There were so many books to read, so much music to listen to and learn, so many subjects to cover. I had to hurry through the reading. There was no time to be fanciful. I had to hurry home to my mother and to my job of selling wine. There was no time to be lost during the summers. During the summers I worked as a playground director. Another summer, following the hasty taking of a Civil Service examination, I got the job of teaching Venetian ironwork to summer students. On Saturdays and evenings I worked as a salesman for Brill Brothers, haberdashers.

It is only now, in the quiet midnight hour as I write this, that I can stop long enough to gather together the details of the headlong rush of those days.

It was the summer of 1906. I had just been graduated from high school, and before me stretched the summer, at the end of which I was to enter college. One job was done, another yet to begin. Less than a week after graduation, as I walked into the post office to mail a letter, I noticed that the Board of Education had posted a list of job opportunities. As I glanced down the list, I saw there was an opening for playground director. I had played basketball and volleyball at high school and convinced myself at once that I was fully qualified. I applied to the Board of Education and got the job. It never occurred to me that I could take these few months and spend them carelessly, like coins which had been given to me.

The basement of Public School 84 at Christopher

and Belmont Avenues was the "playground"; the hours, nine to three o'clock; the number of children, fifty; ages ranging from eight to sixteen—all boys. When I reported to work the first day I found there was no routine, no compulsory attendance, and little, if any, discipline. The boys drifted in and out of the "playground" without leave and without question. There was a little bullying of the youngsters by the older boys, a fist-fight now and then, but on the whole, as I remember it now, we all had fun. I was not much older than many of the boys who attended.

But there was one vital difference which led the boys to accord me authority, which I neither possessed nor felt. I was American; they were immigrant boys newly arrived in this country. I was teaching American games and American slang and helping them to rub off some of their differences. To them I was "teacher" and a hero. I remember the first time an eight-year-old called out across the basement, "Hi, feller." The rest of them broke into a glad shout and applauded; one of them was talking "American."

Before long, the parents of these children began coming in to see me, discussing with me the dreams they had fashioned for their children. In retrospect it seems that every problem they talked about related to how they and their children could be more "American." What food do "Americans" serve at a party? Should Joey learn his father's trade of pastrymaker?

41

Was that "American" enough. Should Mrs. Krolowsky take in boarders? What is a good "American" birthday present? I wonder now how, at eighteen, I had the good sense to treat these questions with the same kind of earnestness with which they were asked.

The gratitude of the boys and their parents followed me for many years. I meet some of these boys now from time to time, and it is no new experience for me to hear them tell how they voted for me and how they worked in the neighborhood for my election.

One boy I remember particularly. He had been hurt in a basketball game and I had carried him to the nearest drugstore. I placed him on two chairs and put my coat over him. I called an ambulance and accompanied him to the hospital. Each day I went to see him. After he left the hospital, I no longer saw him. Many years later, when I was practicing law, he came to see me. He told me that he had prospered and that now, needing the services of a lawyer, had sought me out. He told me that after he had gotten well, he had vowed that he would make no effort to see me until he found some concrete way in which to thank me.

I remember once, when we were playing baseball, one of the boys made such a wild pitch that the ball smashed into a window of a small tailor shop across from the school. Much as I dreaded it, I had no recourse but to brave the wrath of the tailor. Small and shrivelled, the tailor stood before me, waving his arms

42

wildly about and screaming: "Those good-for-noth-ings! What are they doing playing ball anyway? They should be in chedder (Hebrew school), learning the *Torah*. Is this what America teaches them—breaking people's windows?" On and on he went. How I calmed him I don't know. I did, finally. I begged him to come back to the school with me to watch the children play-ing. I tried to explain that in America playing was one of the natural birthrights of all children, rich or poor. What I said must have touched him, perhaps bringing to his memory the youth that had known no play and no fun. I talked for an hour or so and left. The next day I went in to see him again, bringing him a jacket to be mended. "Will you come and see the children?" I asked. Maybe because I returned, or maybe because he had thought of all the things I had said the day before, he came with me. He watched the children playing and said nothing. He left, still having said no word. Fifteen minutes later he returned and shyly offered me the package he was carrying. In it was a shiny, new baseball.

Unaware, of course, I had learned more than the boys did.

The following summer, at the close of my freshman year, I made straight for that post office and glanced down the list that had again been posted. This time there was listed a vacancy, for the teaching of Vene-tian ironwork. I turned away from that list and headed for the public library to get a book or two on what appeared to me a difficult art. It wasn't. I found, after reading closely for about an hour, it was work done with aluminum strips, solder, wire and pliers. The objective was to coil the aluminum strips into fanciful figures, fashioning candelabra, vases, plates, ash receivers, picture frames. The next day I applied at the Board of Education for the position, convincing them that I was adept at this kind of scrollwork. Again I was appointed to Public School 84. Actually, I found I was quite fascinated with Venetian ironwork and learned along with the boys. It would never have done for me to crow with each piece I completed, but whether the pupils or "teacher" was having more fun was a tossup. Today, when I sit with my grandchildren, making odd little figures of aluminum strips, I still don't know who finds the greater amusement, they or I.

About a year ago I returned to Public School 84 as a guest speaker for the Parent-Teachers Association. The meeting was held in the basement of the school which had been the "playground." The dank walls were peeling, plaster hung from the ceiling, the toilets were in an unsightly condition. Not all has been progress.

At Brill Brothers, haberdashers, I started as stockboy and was promoted to salesman. I call them "haberdashers"; the sign said, "Brill Brothers—Gents' Furnishings." Evenings and Saturdays I reported to the store at Broadway and Warren Street to earn my $1.50, selling as many collars and ties and shirts as I could. This was the day of the stiff collar. Our instructions were clear: If a customer came in for a collar, we were practically to bar the exit until he bought the tie along with it. The same procedure was to be followed if all the poor customer wanted was a tie.

One rainy Saturday, a man walked in, clutching his overcoat collar so that his neck was completely covered. He wanted a collar, he told me. Selling him the collar was very simple. Then I proceeded to follow the sales instruction. I showed him all our tie patterns. I modeled them for him. I held them the long way and the broad way. I did practically everything but turn somersaults. But all the man did was stand by and watch me with a kindly smile on his face. Finally, in my desperation, I reached the stage where I no longer spoke but snarled. Still smiling kindly, he asked, "What's your name, son? Mine's Father Corrigan."

So it went. I plodded from one task to the next. I never stopped to allow the flavor of college to permeate—that is, the give-and-take in play, in bull sessions, in the discussions of books, or the dissection of universal problems. I knew that I was going on to law school all during the college days, so my goal was always just ahead of me. The choice of law was my parents', not mine. It was all part of the picture of "making good."

The one person I remember with the greatest clarity

was Columbia's Dean Stone, later Justice of the Supreme Court. I used to try to imitate him. Even now, as I make a speech, I keep before me the picture of this man, self-contained, proceeding with logic from one thought to the next. I never succeed. When I find myself beginning to gesticulate or pound, in order to mark some thought, I sometimes stop in the middle of a sentence, trying to resume with the calm that had impressed me in Dean Stone. I know now that it was not his manner of presentation that excited me. I did not recognize then what I recognize now. It was the excitement of thought, the precision and the logic with which he drove home the points he wished to make.

Because I never stopped to linger over books, it seems to me that I remain always book-hungry. Time had crowded so much into my life, and yet crowded so much out of it, that the race still goes on. I have long since abandoned the violin which I once played. But I have taught myself to play the piano. Between books and the piano I snatch the rare moments when time stands still. And there is always the opera. For the past 25 years Stella and I have had the same seats at the Metropolitan, attending the Saturday evening performances of each season.

As far back as I can remember, every Friday night was family night. Aunts, uncles, cousins, many and voluble, came in by two's, three's, and singly. No invitations were issued; none was needed. Only those who were coming for dinner bothered to tell Mother about it a day or two before. Our house was the center of the family. These Friday nights were invested with a warmth that has carried itself forward into every Friday night of my life. Friday nights are nights set apart. I have not been home many Friday nights in the past two decades. If the legislative program permitted me to leave Washington and get home for the weekend, there were other duties and other responsibilities to be met—speeches, conferences, meetings with delegations of constituents, the whole range of pressures which surround the Congressman when he is presumably not at work. But whether in or out of the house on Friday nights, the magic about it persists.

Into this family night were drawn my friends and those of my brother and sisters as well. Part of the evening was just talk, sometimes there were games—charades, musical chairs, "ghosts" and various forms of "twenty questions." But always there was music.

Mother and father had no formal musical education, but their interest in music was so avid that their children could not have escaped it had they tried. Every third Monday of the season was opera night for Mother and Father. When I was a small child, I used to ask my mother every Monday, "Is this 'dress up night'?" "Dress-up night" was opera night. Dinner was hurried, a flush of excitement was on mother's face, and my father seemed to grow two inches taller. When they were dressed in their finery, they stood before us for inspection. We were always pleased and proud of them on "dress-up night."

My mother's favorite operas became mine—*La Traviata, Il Trovatore, Aïda*. A Verdi-worshiper, my father called her. There was talk of Patti, Caruso, Eames, Jean de Reszke. Father played the piano by ear. My brother and sisters, who diligently practiced the piano each day, would stand by completely humbled, watching my father's fingers flying over the keyboard, without any music before him. He used to say, "You call the tune and I'll play it."

My mother and father had both decided that I was to be the violinist of the household. I rebelled against the violin and against practicing, but I never succeeded in getting out of it. Practice I must and practice I did. My lessons began when I was ten years old. By the time I was sixteen I was sufficiently proficient to give violin lessons to children in the neighborhood. But I was never more than just proficient. I had always wanted to play the piano, but the family needed a violinist; so there I was.

Thus the memories flow one into the other, some obscured, some heightened by the crowded years. As I look back, I realize how I moved in a straight line, steadily, even doggedly, from goal to goal, looking always to the next step.

At the age of twenty-four I became a lawyer, but I did not abandon the wine route. I had prospered as a wine salesman; I was not so certain of my future in the law. I began my law practice with Meyer Krashauer at 51 Chambers Street, New York City. My first clients were my wine customers.

I was now "in a position" to marry, to settle down, as we say in Brooklyn. I believed it, Stella believed it, but Stella's mother did not. "For seven years I have been courting your daughter," I told Mrs. Baar, "and each time I talk about marriage you keep telling me there is time." One evening as I watched the disapproving eyes of Mrs. Baar watching Stella and myself, I turned abruptly to her and said, "Do you want a wedding or an elopement?" (For many years after that Stella used to mimic the fury of my voice at that moment.) The only reply Mrs. Baar could make in face of the attack was, "Very well, then!" Her fury was no less than mine.

That very night the date was set. We were to be married in three weeks—June 30, 1914. After seven years of "going together" Stella and I found ourselves rushing at headlong pace to get ready for the wedding. Mrs. Baar saw in the occasion no need for elaborate joy-making. It was a small wedding. There were sixty guests, mostly the family and a few old friends. Just before the ceremony, I turned to Stella and asked,

"What kind of bridegroom do I make?" "Nervous," she said and laughed aloud.

We had found a 4-room apartment in a 4-story walkup; kitchen, dining room, living room, and bedroom. The rent was $35 a month. It was the right background for "so they were married and lived happily ever after." The house was on Caton Avenue near East 17th Street. No part of Brooklyn was more gracious.

Two evenings a week we set aside for the study of Italian. Although, one by one, my wine customers were turning into clients, I was not fully prepared to disassociate myself from the wine route altogether. Within a year or two, however, I found that I could afford to abandon the route forever.

On March 17, 1917 our daughter Jane was born. A handsome child, Jane soon developed a lusty independence of her own. She was my champion and my defender. When I went to Congress, her first preoccupation was to make converts of all her schoolmates to the Democratic Party. She constituted herself a committee of one "For the Re-election of Emanuel Celler." At election time she would charge headlong into the fray, sparing neither herself nor her adversaries. When she was about nine, there was a battle royal. After school the boys would cover the blackboard with slogans for the Republican candidate. Early the next morning Jane would appear before class began and set about the work of erasing. Onto the blackboard would go slogans for the Democratic Party. This became a chase. The teachers erased the blackboard; after school the boys would begin the campaign again; and before school Jane would revise the political advertisements. Sometimes Jane would not wait for the morning, but would hide behind the school watching for the boys to leave so she could rush in to do her political work. This went on for about two weeks before election day. She got no assist. She was one girl (Democrat) against six boys (Republican).

Soon after I was elected to Congress, I took Jane for her first visit to Washington. When we got to the White House, Jane stood at the foot of the staircase and told the guard, "Now I want to see where the President sleeps." "No," said the guard; "if you want to see the bedroom you must get a special letter from your Congressman." With all the scorn a five-year-old can muster, Jane replied: "Don't be silly; that's only my father."

"Downright Jane," I called her. I remember that when Jane, in her senior year at Wellesley, came home during the Easter recess, I asked her, "Now that your graduation is so near, what would you like to do after you get out of college? What would you like to be?" The question, so characteristic of me, was met by the Jane who always knew her own mind and spoke it. "If it's all the same to you," she replied, "I'd like to

51

graduate in June, meet a grand fellow, and marry him in October." So it happened—except that she was married in November.

Four years after Jane's birth, our second daughter, Judy, was born. How shall I tell you about Judy? Judy was born a spastic paraplegic, with paralysis of her legs and arms. Nothing of the mind was affected, and her intelligence shone out of her eyes, set in a face that was as lovely as Jane's. Stella and I determined that at no time would Judy be treated any differently from the rest of us. She would eat with us, play with us, and talk with us as all children do with their parents. Because of this, Jane's sturdiness was not a thing to be quarreled with.

There were tutors in the house to give Judy her schooling from grade school through college. Judy and I throughout these years have talked and talked and talked—talked of the books she had read and I never did; talked of the music she learned more profoundly than I could ever learn. We talked of politics and of metaphysics. We explored the soul and the "why" of pain. And we laughed together. I had fallen into the habit of drawing little pictures on post cards and mailing them to the family whenever I was away from home. I remembered all the funny incidents so that I could come home and laugh with Judy over them. If I would strike a pious attitude about the sins of management against labor, Judy would draw me away from the easy generalizations. Our subjects ranged from prison reform to the comic genius of Chekhov.

Only the other day Judy showed me a letter of mine she had saved for eleven years:

MENDEL BILKIE
   Soldiers' Home
     BATTLEBORO, Vermont
                    June 3, 1941
My dear Miss Celler:

I have just learned, confidentially, that you have a close friend who is an international spy. I got this straight from the horse's mouth—J. Edgar Hoover. He usually visits our Soldiers' Home, for suspects. He got the information, steppe by steppe, from the Russian OGPU. Confirmation has been assured by the A.P.—U.P.—C.O.D.—I.O.U.—T.O.T.—and P. M. I have yet to hear from A.M.

TAKE WARNING - - - - - - YOU ARE A SUSPECT!

Your friend is Dotty Lamour Toujour Cube-ie. She is in the employ of Rashid Ali Beg Galiani, who was recently chased out of Bagdad by the English. She is also conspiring with that bloodhound of Beirut, Fawjiel Kaoughibey and Foreign Minister Yosuki Matsouka, to steal the oil wells of Persia. She believes that oils well that ends well. Dotty has been very conspicuous in the Near Yeast. She has been seen carousing and night-clubbing with Algerians, Moroccans, Arabs,

53

Croats, Turks, Iraquis, Syrians and others from the Near Yeast. Soon it will be the Far Yeast. Then, Fleischmann's.

A few months ago they found her doing the rhumba with Mahatma Gandhi. He liked it so well, he said Dotty could have his shirt—I mean, his sheet.

Then she got over to Chungking and beguiled the officials there with stories. She made a jitter-bug out of Generalissimo Chiang Kai-Shek. She told him the following story. 'What is it that a little dog does and a man steps in?' . . . . He didn't know the answer, which is, of course . . . pants. The Soong sisters were outraged and they ordered her out of China.

It is said that she is responsible for the Hess-capade.

Her latest is to bring Ulster and Ireland together—for a hell of a scrap with brickbats. Irish confetti, in other words.

Informed rumor has it that she has taken Elena Lupescu's place at ex-King Carol's side.

I hope you will visit us soon at the Soldiers' Home. However, I am warning you—you better watch your step with Dotty or you'll find yourself in a . . . well, just watch out . . . it *won't* be a sarong!   I am, fraternally yours,

(signed) Mendel Bilkie

So it has been these many years—this jest to hide the pain, and the worlds within worlds of ideas.

I call them "my little harem"—Stella and Jane and Judy. I have said this so many times that now I get an indulgent, pitying smile when I use the expression. They are women of independence of thought, sensitive and perceptive, and very often they just "put up with me." My wife once told me that while she was upstairs with Judy and I was entertaining below, Judy said, "Daddy must have gotten some new friends; I hear him telling that same old story again."

After Judy's birth the apartment was too small to hold the four of us and the special nurse for Judy. We moved to our own home at 303 MacDonough Street, and there we lived for twenty-six years. It was a brownstone home, very much in the elegance of its day with its three floors—the living quarters on the lowest level, the formal parlor on the second floor, and the bedrooms on the third.

How many hundreds of feet have shuffled, marched, stamped and dragged through that living room on the ground floor I could never count. After March 4, 1923, I no longer entered the house as husband and father only, because along with me came the incessant ringing of the telephone, the constant ring of the doorbell, the knock of the special delivery postman, and the cry of "Western Union—telegram." I was now Congressman.

Sundays were "court" days. The door was left un-latched so that constituents could enter without ring-ing or knocking. Beginning with the year 1930, the stream of visitors seemed never to end as the jobs grew fewer and fewer. Many came into the house desperate for a few dollars for the week's groceries. I had found it necessary to provide myself with a stack of dollar bills because I had learned I could not withstand so many of the moving stories I had come to expect. Old men and young men—hat in hand—stood before me, not for charity but for jobs.

In the years before the depression the story had been different. Like my experiences at the playground, they were concerned mostly with the adjustment of the alien to the America which was new to him. One day an Italian immigrant came with his little seven-year-old girl. His wife had died and he was trying to bring up four youngsters. The little girl had been sent home from school because she had, he told me, "bugs in her head." The teacher was lying, of course; he would have it no other way. Half in English and half in Italian he begged me to undo this injustice and disgrace to his family name and honor. I told him to keep his girl out of school for a few days, to wash and fine-comb her hair each night, and then to return to me the following Sunday. He did and, grinning broadly and proudly, he said that his daughter had gone back to school on the previous Thursday and that she had been allowed to stay. He seized both my hands, repeating at least three times, "You are better than a doctor."

In the years before 1930 it had been possible for us to think of ourselves as a closely-knit family group. My journeys to Washington were still not so extended that we could not think of our life together as experiences shared. Dinner for us was the hour of competition—who could tell the funniest story? There were visitors and visiting, the opera and the theater, for all of us. From none of this was Judy, despite her handicap and her wheel chair, ever excluded.

As the pace in Washington grew swifter and swifter, beginning with the Roosevelt era and continuing through the rise of totalitarianism to the second World War and to that period after of neither war nor peace, the road home stretched longer and longer. Four or five days of the week were spent in Washington, the remaining days at home in Brooklyn or in my law office. These competed for my attention with the speeches that had to be made in and out of the district, the legislative homework, the intruding jangle of the telephone and the troubled needs of my constituents.

My family and friends accepted the pattern. Visiting, the theater, the dinner parties became interludes between one job that had just been finished and another about to be done. Could this life have been lived differently? Is it I, or the work I have chosen?

The house is quiet as I write this. Judy is asleep. Jane, married now for thirteen years, together with her two children—Sue, nine, and Jill, five—and her husband Sydney, had joined us for dinner. They have gone home and with them have gone the bubble and the merriment and the little tricks with matches and napkins which send the children into gales of laughter. Stella and I are sitting alone in the handsome, wide living room of the apartment which Stella has furnished with quiet and distinctive taste—Stella sitting there in the big chair, looking ahead and dreaming what dream I do not know. I feel impelled to mar that silence.

"Stella," I say, bringing her back to me; "Stella, do you remember my first law case?" For a moment her face is blank, but then she breaks into a long laugh.

"Do I! Don't you remember, you got twenty-five dollars for defending the Polish man who had voted without being a citizen. He thought he was. I remember when I came into the courtroom—I couldn't let you try your first case without being there—I found myself taking a seat among the client's family and friends. They didn't know me. One man looked around and asked, 'Who's the lawyer?' Another man answered, 'A Mr. Celler,' and pointed to you. The first man didn't look happy about it. He frowned and said, 'What, that kid!'

58

"I paid more attention to them than I did to you. I was so nervous, I kept scratching my leg and ended up with a tremendous hole in my stocking. I didn't even hear the judge say 'Case dismissed.' I was so busy beaming back at the beaming faces around me.

"But I did hear some of the terrible things the lawyer on the opposing side said about you and your client. I was incensed. When the case was over, just before lunchtime, that lawyer who said those terrible things about you—do you remember?—put his arm across your shoulder and asked you to go to lunch with him. And when you said you would, I pulled you aside and demanded to know 'How can you be so friendly with that man when he said such awful things about you?' "

Stella and I both laughed at her telling of the story. It brought to mind the men with whom I had worked in the practice of law, the men who had been my partners, with the firm of Kaufman, Weitzner and Celler, and then, after 1936, the firm of Weisman, Celler, Quinn, Allan, and Spett.

I did well in the law those first years, going along from case to case, fighting down the restlessness in me. For ten years I fought that restlessness. One day James J. Sexton, then Tax Commissioner of New York City, came to me and asked me if I would be willing to be the Democratic candidate for the then Tenth Congressional District of New York (later the Fifteenth

59

and now the Eleventh Congressional District). The seat was then held by Dr. Lester Volk, a Republican, who had won it in a special election and was seeking re-election. Commissioner Sexton told me that, as I knew, of course, the district had never gone Democratic, but here was an opportunity for someone of energy and aggressiveness to turn the district into a Democratic stronghold.

I learned subsequently that he offered the nomination to me because no one else wanted it. "A Democrat didn't have a chance," was the popular belief. I believed so, too; I didn't have a chance. But it was worth a try, if only for the fact of the excitement it stirred up in me, and for the experience that comes with running for public office. Stella didn't want me to accept the nomination. She knew then what has been borne out by these many years in Congress—that it meant the end of a personal life and the many personal satisfactions that go with it. It meant loneliness for her and loneliness for me, in my being away from home for long stretches of time. Stella could not come with me to Washington because Judy needed her at home.

Only two men said I could win. One was Hymie Shorenstein, then Democratic leader and later Recorder of Deeds for the Borough of Brooklyn. Hymie was shrewd; he knew his people of Brooklyn. He knew their problems and their struggles better than any trained sociologist, although Hymie could neither read nor write. Everybody knew Hymie and respected him. It is still a name that can conjure up endless stories in Brooklyn households, neighborly stories, spiced with homely humor, which bespeak the affection in which he was held.

The other was Aaron L. Jacoby, now Chief Clerk of the Surrogate's Court of the Borough of Brooklyn. If I were asked to define the word "friendship," surely there would be none other to whom I could more directly point as its embodiment than Aaron. We have held together these many years. I believe he knows me as no other man knows me. He has never asked me to be other than what I am, accepting me as I am, with all the revelations of weaknesses and cracks in my armor that showed through the years. The sharp twinkle of his eye, contrasting with the calm deliberation of his speech, gives evidence of a man who judges, but who judges without self-righteousness.

Armed only with the encouragement of these two men, I entered the race. I did not ask the party organization for help. It was ill-advised for it to spend time and money in a district where there was, so it seemed, no chance of winning. I gathered my personal friends and relatives around me. I organized the district on a precinct basis and assigned a friend or a relative to each such precinct. A friend of mine donated to me rent-free a building on Ralph Avenue between Monroe and Madison Streets. We almost drowned in a barrage of rulers and blotters which other friends had printed for me. These I had distributed in all the public schools. I hired sound-trucks and drove from street corner to street corner, making speeches. It was not uncommon for my opponent to be on one side of the street while I was on the other, each of us trying to out-shout the other.

The Republicans had been at the helm in the district for so long that it seemed only logical for me to adopt the slogan: "It's time for a change." (Shades of 1952!) Mostly I talked about the danger of complacency, of apathy, of indifference, and more particularly of the evils of prohibition and the virtues of the League of Nations. Every night there were five or six speeches. I worked, Stella worked, my sisters and my cousins and my brother and my aunts worked. One friend of mine in the chocolate business gave me what seemed to be tons of cocoa. We put it up in tins and sent one to every household in the district. Maybe I couldn't win, but I could try.

Despite the certainty of everybody that I couldn't win, excepting, of course, always Hymie Shorenstein and Aaron Jacoby, I waited out that election day in November of 1922 in an agony of suspense. I guess I really believed, deep down inside of me, that I could make it. I did. I won by a margin of 3,111 votes.

Thirty years later, in 1952, I was elected by a vote of 125,892, as against my opponent's 36,805. Today the Republican candidacy for the district is the challenge, as was the Democratic candidacy in 1922.

Chapter Five

If to do were as easy as to know what were good to do, chapels had been churches, and poor men's cottages princes' palaces.
— Shakespeare: *The Merchant of Venice*

I am including here what I wrote down on July 28, 1952, immediately after my return from the Democratic Convention:

"I want to put this down now while the impressions are still fresh and before I yield to the temptations of hindsight. This is July 28, 1952. I have just returned from the Democratic National Convention held in Chicago. As a delegate from Brooklyn and as a member of the Committee on Platform and Resolutions, I had come to Chicago a few days earlier to listen to the testimony that would be given to the subcommittee of that committee. With the pouring in of the delegates on Saturday and Sunday for the opening day, July 21, the outstanding emotion was bewilderment. There were many who didn't dare to state their conviction or choice for the Presidential nominee. These were people afraid not to be on the winning side. They wanted to be herded into groups, primed, and prompted. Many, who came instructed to vote for a nominee, expressed greater assurance, but through that expression ran a wavering thread of fear lest, in the final count, they not be found among the winners.

"The most dedicated were the Kefauver supporters. It was a touching earnestness, this atmosphere of the white charger and the white plume that these had drawn around themselves. But there was, too, a bit of pathos and a bit of irony and a bit of humor in the self-righteousness with which they politicked, as if they alone knew and could proclaim the truth.

"Here, again, we have the contrast of the public man and the private man. I have known Estes Kefauver for many years. We were both members of the Committee on the Judiciary in the House of Representatives. The members of the Committee had grown to respect Estes Kefauver for his application, for his studious approach to problems, for his retreat from publicity, and for his lack of dogmatism. Before the Senate Crime Committee, of which he was Chairman, thrust him forward into the public eye, I should have said of him, "He is a quiet man, and thoughtful."

"So it was with the other leading contenders for the Presidential nomination—a study in contrast between what each man is and what each man appeared to be. About Mr. Averell Harriman there was a curious lack of excitement. There were few who were either passionately attached or passionately averse to him. In this instance, the public portrait that emerged gave no indication of the solidity and the strength that is Mr. Harriman's. His ability as an administrator and his drive, which had led him straight to the heart of many intricate problems, never came through.

"Senator Russell, while held captive by regional interests which claimed him as their own, was most effective in presenting a merger of the public and the private man. Of all the candidates it was Senator Russell who suffered least from self-consciousness; who did not permit his supporters to obscure the portrait of the man he is. He stated his position unequivocally so that it was clearly understood, and as much as the South fervently claimed him for themselves, he was able to prove, through his directness, that his was a candidacy above regional interests. This is no mean achievement for a man during the heat of partisan debate and the clutching for the prize.

"The convention has been stigmatized characteristically as a medium for the jockeying for position and for the realization of ambition and prestige. This is true, but only in the most limited sense. As in 1948, I was again a member of the Committee on Platform and Resolutions. The television camera never poked its way, then or now, into the crowded room where the platform was being fought over, ripped apart sentence by sentence, and then sewn up again. Of that I am glad. There are some places where television does not belong, and this is one of them. There were in that room men and women who, uninhibited and relieved of the anxiety to "look good" on television, could speak their minds, without fear of losing favor with this or that group. And while emotions ran high in that room, they were emotions profound and fundamental. I sincerely hope I am believed when I say that into the shaping of the platform, both in 1948 and in 1952, went more than just the weaving of a net to catch the vote. It was the hammering out of the philosophy of government. It was the continuance of a debate that started with the writing of the Articles of Confederation in 1781.

"There were actually three large groups:

"One group believed passionately that the welfare of the people of the country demanded that the Federal Government take the fullest share of responsibility in the welfare of its people; that powers be centralized in the national government, viewing state lines mostly in the geographical sense. It was their conviction that federal action primarily could secure to the people the abundant life.

"The second group—the moderates, so-called—argued with as much conviction that the Federal Government intervene only where the States themselves had failed to secure these rights. These asked for a greater measure of responsibility for the States themselves, so that on a local level constituents may participate more fully in gaining the benefits to be sought.

"Then there was the third group, the group called "States' Righters," who vehemently argued that the Constitution demanded that only such powers as are specifically and clearly delegated belong to the Federal Government; the rest are reserved for the States.

"I am talking, of course, of the groups as they formed themselves at the convention. While these general groups also exist in the Congress, the lines are not so clearly drawn there. There is much crossing over, but these outlines are never completely erased.

"The first group cried that the third group was for a Balkanization of the United States. The third group cried that the first group was guilty of the heinous crime of socialism. The second group stood between the two, now taking sides with the one, now with the other; a buffer, a negotiator, a compromiser, and to both the others—to use a word that has fallen into ill repute—an appeaser.

"All these passions, these convictions, had been poured into one issue—civil rights. It had become the rod upon which each group raised its flag. There were those of the South who used the civil rights issue to cater to a frightened and often vicious element of their constituency to carry them to political prominence. And there were others in the South who saw in states' rights a clarification of their position to preserve the integrity of the States as political units. There were those in the North who used the civil rights issue as the trade-mark of liberalism, to be used to propel themselves as individuals into power. But there were those, also, who fundamentally saw in the civil rights issue the eternal fight for individual dignity, for the granting of equality of opportunity to all peoples.

"But in that committee room the demagoguery was dropped, and the fundamental concepts, though passionately argued, stood there in their nakedness for reexamination.

"As in 1948, so in 1952, my experiences in that room renewed my faith, not only in the intellectual content of our country, but in the heart of the country as well. It was exciting—the sound of ideas clashing, dividing, and meeting again, truly in the name of the welfare of the people. Had the people been witness to what was said in that room, both in 1948 and in 1952, it could not be said, as so often and so glibly it is said, "Politics is a dirty game."

"Where did I stand in this foray? As I think it over, I conclude that I stood with all three, judging each issue by itself and as it affected the nation as a whole. I could not impose upon myself a rigidity that would chain me irrevocably to one group only. It seems to me that each issue, as each individual, must be judged on its own and then put into the context of the whole.

"I was not satisfied, and still am not, with the civil rights plank. I wanted the words to be capable of single definition only, so clear that their meaning would be unmistakable. The civil rights issue addresses itself, not only to the South, but to the North. It is not only the "For Whites Only" signs, the symbol of segregation and degradation of the Negro in the South, which bitterly offend and from which I instinctively recoil whenever I see them. My heart curls into a tight ball when I walk down some streets in Brooklyn and watch the little colored children playing with their jacks and skipping rope in the streets, with their big, black, innocent eyes looking up at me. I look from them to the houses in which, by social fiat, they must live. I think of the doors closed to them, in training, in job opportunities, in labor unions and by trade associations. My guilt crawls inside of me because I have not done enough, because I can never do enough for people whom society punishes for no reason but the color of their skin. I have no room in my heart for any temperance toward the degradation and despoiling of human dignity.

"When a constituent comes to me and says that a job is denied him because he is a Catholic or a Jew, it becomes my intolerable burden. Need we stand helpless before these conditions? So I fought for a stronger

71

civil rights plank, and I lost. Maybe it is well that I did. Maybe my emotions blinded me to the fact that perhaps that which is achieved step by step stays with us always and gradually gains an acceptance no political wind can overturn. I do not know.

"I fought in another area—this time it was with the New York delegation. The New York delegation had come to the convention committed to support the candidacy of Averell Harriman. We knew by the end of the first ballot (and before) that Harriman could not at any time summon sufficient strength to win the nomination. New York had 94 votes, the largest of any State delegation, and throwing that strength in one direction or another could start the ball rolling toward the convention's final choice. I wanted Stevenson. I said so. I had witnessed a phenomenon and I refused to close my eyes to it for the sake of political bargaining. When I first came to Chicago, days before the convention opened, I heard the delegates around me saying wistfully, 'If only Stevenson would run!' While they respected the caliber of the leading contenders (and upon this the Democratic Party must commend itself), they had a sense of vagueness and drifting. 'All good men, yes; and yet . . .'

"As I write this, I do not know what the outcome will be in November. I knew, however, that when Governor Stevenson had finished his welcoming address an electric shock ran through the delegation. I

72

did not know then that it had also run through the country. No platitudes, no 'oratory.' There was a feeling of exultation that before us was a man of stature. After the speech, the delegates turned to each other saying, 'He's *the* man!' I don't know how many times I heard that.

"Among my fellow delegates I argued for Stevenson. Over and above the necessity to 'pick a winner,' I was arguing against mediocrity, against the pall and the restlessness that mediocrity brings with it. I relived, in the moments while I was arguing, the tenseness, the excitement, the unraveling of new ideas, the courage to dare and do which characterized Washington during the early years of the Roosevelt Administration. I argued for the future, too; for literacy and for wisdom in the conduct of world affairs at a time when a troubled world trembled on a precipice. I lost.

"On the second ballot the New York delegation stayed with Harriman, but I balked. I was not talking in derogation of Harriman and this they knew. At the end of the second ballot I was not a popular fellow with my State delegates, though I had voted with them. I had stated at that time that I would refuse to vote for anyone but Stevenson on the third ballot.

"On the third ballot the New York delegation threw its strength to Stevenson. This holding out by the New York delegation was actually the measure of defiance against the South. Would throwing their strength to

Stevenson be interpreted as a capitulation to a candidate acceptable to all elements of the convention? And if a candidate is acceptable to all elements, can it not, therefore, be interpreted as a retreat of the liberals?

"I can understand this attitude. It is difficult to describe the frustration that seizes one when time and again legislation is brought to the floor and the coalition of Southern Democrats and Republicans beats it down. Then party responsibility does not exist. Legislation on housing, on controls, legislation which derives from the party platform arrived at in its convention in 1948 and on which the Democratic Party made its national bid in 1948, and won, is fought bitterly and successfully by such a coalition. You battle every inch of the way, and each legislative victory is gained only through the nerve-racking battle against members of your own party. And this legislative climate is aggravated by the suspicion each group has of the other. As Chairman of the Committee on the Judiciary, I rise on the floor to lead the discussion on a bill, and since this gentleman from New York carries the label 'liberal,' a number of the Southern Representatives are immediately 'on guard.' So is it when a Representative from Mississippi or South Carolina rises; the liberals are on guard. In most instances these bills, particularly bills coming from the Committee on the Judiciary, are not invested with sectional interests, but

74

it is sometimes amusing to see both sides tense up, ready to spring into action.

"It was easy, then, to understand why at Chicago the New York delegation refused to bow to what I termed the inevitable. They could see as easily as I the caliber of the man. They had been ready, even before the convention opened, to accept Governor Stevenson. They had hoped, in the months following President Truman's announcement that he would not run again, that Stevenson would consent to carry the standard for the Democratic Party. But when Stevenson was tagged as acceptable to all segments of the convention, all the suspicions and fears came into operation.

"Stevenson was not a compromise candidate. He was never offered as one or sold as one, as was President Truman in the 1944 convention when Truman was put forward as the Vice-Presidential nominee in place of Wallace. Stevenson was not put forward, nor did I support Stevenson at any time, simply because he was a moderator to temper this faction or that. Nobody with any reflection at all could place him in the category of compromise candidates like Harding for the Republicans or Cox for the Democrats. It was not for the interest of party unity either. It was because he stood head and shoulders above any man who had appeared on the national scene.

"When I returned from Chicago, I found that with two speeches—the speech of welcome and the speech of acceptance—Governor Stevenson had stridden across a continent. I have never known anything like this to happen before. In this you could see the hunger of the people for honesty and clarity, for literacy, for humility, for wit, for pride in a man who could represent them before the entire world, standing in cultural equality with the practised diplomats of Europe and Asia. I have found our conduct of foreign affairs suffers much from the feeling of inferiority our people and our diplomats bring with them to these operations. The charges of materialism hurled against us by both the friendly and the hostile nations of the world have almost convinced us that we are lacking in finesse and subtlety and are not quite capable of the adroit maneuvers of which foreign diplomats appear to be the masters. We have lost many a diplomatic skirmish because of this kind of insecurity. The reception given to Governor Stevenson's two speeches could not make it clearer.

"I will let this stand. Governor Adlai Stevenson will be the next President of these United States."

I had not thought that any postscript would be necessary. Such had been my estimate of Adlai Stevenson at the convention. It was not changed throughout the campaign of 1952. My admiration for Governor Stevenson was by no means a diminution of the qualities of President-elect Dwight D. Eisenhower. My positive prediction proves that in addition to the two certainties of death and taxes there is another—the certainty that no man can be certain.

> "Of that there is no manner of doubt—
> No probable, possible shadow of doubt—
> No possible doubt whatever."

Chapter Six

When thou cuttest down thine harvest in thy field, and hast forgot a sheaf in the field, thou shalt not go again to fetch it; it shall be for the stranger, for the fatherless, and for the widow . . .

Deuteronomy, 24:19

One of the grossest exaggerations in political history is to place the blame or the garland for some act on a "handful of willful men." To believe that is to believe that people are automatons, wooden puppets manipulated by the force of certain personalities. There are ruthlessly ambitious men and men of good will who have exerted incalculable influence upon the people. This is true. But I maintain that only if the people provide for them a climate of acceptance first can their influences take root.

Nowhere is this more clearly demonstrated than in the work of the Congress of the United States. For thirty years I have watched this interaction in Congress. My first bitter shock came with the first really big debate on the floor of the House in which I participated. This was on the Johnson Immigration Act in the spring of 1924. It was in that Act that the "na-

79

tional origins" theory of immigration became entrenched in the body of our immigration law. It was a theory which said that the Nordic was superior to any other national group. The bill under debate called for the yearly admission of 161,184 immigrants to come from all of Europe, but of that number 131,937 would be allowed to come from Great Britain and Germany, from Scandinavia (Norway, Sweden, Denmark, Iceland), The Netherlands and Switzerland, leaving for the entire remaining countries of Europe only 29,247.

The debate on the bill was long, passionate, and bitter. I believe that not in the three decades I have been in Congress have I heard such venom spilled on the floor of the House.

One member rose to say: "We have admitted the dregs of Europe until America has been Orientalized, Europeanized, Africanized, and mongrelized to that insidious degree that our genius, stability, greatness, and promise of advancement and achievement are actually menaced."

There was another who rose to proclaim with great vehemence: "The hour has come. It may be even now too late for the white race in America, the English-speaking people, the laborer of high ideals, to assert his superiority in the work of civilization and to save America from the menace of a further immigration of undesirable aliens. I wish it were possible to close our gates against any quota from southern Europe or from the Orientals, the Mongolian countries and the yellow races of men."

And wild applause filled the House.

There were those of us who rose to fight against this tide—Congressmen Sabath, Dickstein, LaGuardia, Jacobstein, myself, and others. The waves of hate grew higher and bolder. "Will the gentleman yield?" I cried again and again. But there was no yielding. When I finally rose to talk, I knew it was in vain. I used every device at my command. I pleaded and I reasoned. I put colored charts on display. By their use I attempted to show our strength in terms of population; how the periods of greatest immigration brought with them greatest economic development.

I pleaded: "Let us at least be truthful. In fact, deception is futile. It is as clear as the sun that the majority of the Immigration Committee and most proponents of this measure like the gentleman from Kansas (Mr. Tincher), who blurted out his true feelings while talking on the bill, do not want the 'wops,' 'dagoes,' 'Hebrews,' 'hunkies,' 'bulls,' and others known by similar epithets. Just so, in 1840, 1850, and 1860 you did not want the 'beery Germans' and 'dirty Irish.' The Germans and Irish were mongrels, self-seekers, disreputable, and would not assimilate. We know now how good a citizenry they have become."

I quoted from Army authorities and from scientific studies which proved indisputably that there was no

higher percentage of mental deficiency, physical dis
abilities and disease, and criminalism among the for
eign-born than among the native. It had been neces
sary to get this on record because again and again
these charges were hurled against them.

I went on to plead:

"It is the most vaunted purpose of the majority
of the Immigration Committee to encourage as-
similation, yet this bill has already done more than
anything I know of to bring about discord among
our resident aliens. Processes have been encouraged that make for the very antithesis of assimi-
lation. The Italian is told he is not wanted; the
Pole is confronted with the stigma of inferiority;
the bar sinister is placed upon the Czech and the
Russian. Fortunate is the one whose cradle was
rocked in Germany or England. The 'inferior
complex' is now extended to all Europe, save
Nordics. The Austrian rubbing elbows with the
Norwegian in the subway or on the street is beset
with emotions of inferiority. His pride surges
within him. He resents the stigma placed upon
him. Surely he does not view the favored one with
complacency. Does he not rather view him with
hatred? Thanks to the ill-considered and improvi-
dent Johnson bill; and so race is set against race,
class against class."

They listened, but did not hear. "The Southern Europeans are bolshevists," members repeated over and over and over again. They were talking about the Slavs and the Poles and the Italians—the people I knew. I had lived with them, gone to school with them, worked with them. They were the people of courage who had left the security of the past and took the brave journey to America with hope for themselves and their children; who had worked to make America richer, creating new industries and new jobs. They were the people who brought their diverse cultures so that the blood stream of America coursed with greater vigor in the arts, in the sciences, and in the skills of mankind.

As I reread in 1952 the words I spoke in 1924, I grew heartsick to know that there are passages in the 1924 immigration debate I had only to lift out to apply them to the immigration debate of 1952:

> The war and the present postwar period, both redolent with hysteria, offer the worst possible background for reasoning out the immigration problem. As a result of the ordeal of the war we are still hysterical about immigration. The ultra restrictionist and those behind the Johnson bill claim we are a disunited people. Nothing is further from the truth. The war proved that of all nations in the combat we were the most united.

We were successful in welding our many peoples without the use of force or coercion. The methods embodied in the Johnson bill are the forceful methods used by Germany to assimilate her people. We know what ill success attended upon Germany's efforts. It is almost inconceivable that we should be adopting the futile German method.

Add the word "cold" before "war" and the words "and the Soviet Union" after "Germany," substitute "McCarran" for "Johnson" and no other word need be changed.

To the charges of radical infiltration among immigrants, I replied:

> "Does not radicalism flourish as well among natives as aliens? Bill Hayward, Eugene V. Debs, and William Foster are Anglo-Saxons. Rhode Island, our most alien State, has the least socialistic vote. The I. W. W. organization is, primarily, a native organization. Nor is radicalism limited to non-Nordics. New Zealand probably has the highest form of State socialism and is peopled almost totally by Nordics. The spread of radicalism is due not to the coming of any particular class of aliens but to industrial discontent. Grinding the faces of workmen, be they native or alien, is the primary cause."

The charges have a familiar, contemporary ring, do hey not?

Those who were less venomous stated categorically, 'We have no room." But there had always been those vho said we had no room. They began saying it in the Colonies, and in the original Thirteen States, and as he nation spread across a continent.

For years I worried and puzzled over that 1924 lebate. What was wrong? Were these men representative? Did their thinking reflect the thinking of the people of the country? Had they taken it upon themselves to write a law contrary not only to the nation's interest—but contrary to the fundamentals of a democracy that stated categorically "all men are created equal"?

As year followed year I came to realize that the Immigration Act was not the work of a group of men apart from the people. It was a product of the temper of the times. It was the same temper which had rejected Wilson and the League of Nations. We, generally, were tired—tired of foreign entanglements. Like children who had been asked to do something for which they were not ready, we wanted to pick up our marbles and go home. The angry quarrels of Europe, the division among its peoples, the never-ending Balkan jealousies, the diplomatic game to make and keep balances of power, represented to the United States a quarrelsome, dangerous, ill-bred family that we did not want to join. We were asking to be children just a little while longer. We expressed this wish in isolationism, in irritability, in the high tariff, in the immigration law of 1917, and in uncurbed credits and real estate booms. It takes a long time to grow up.

If the climate of acceptance does not exist, no strength of personality can force it into being. In 193? President Roosevelt's quarantine speech was met with dismay by the members of Congress and the people. The New Deal reforms of President Roosevelt took hold only because the country was ready for them. No brilliance, no eloquence, for good or for evil, can in a democracy force a position until the people as a whole are ready to embrace it. Let me make it plain. I do not mean that an idea can prevail without leadership. But no plant will grow in a soil which is deficient to receive it.

With the 1924 debate one of my central interests in my work in Congress began.

I was never able to determine how deep was the shock in the heart of the United States at the slaughter of millions throughout the Nazi regime. There were sporadic speeches on the floors of the House and the Senate. There were editorials and there were speeches without end on the subject throughout the country. Yet there was no concerted movement that could have compelled the United States to consider the possibility of opening its doors to those fleeing murder. The de-ate shifted back and forth from the corner of Aid to Britain to the corner of America First.

There were few who followed the proceedings of the Evian Conference in 1938, an international conference called to discuss solutions for those pounding for an open door to escape the extermination camps. There were fewer who followed the proceedings of the Bermuda Conference, called by the United States and Great Britain in April of 1943, to find solutions among the two great democracies where international co-operation had failed.

Where I could obtain the use of radio facilities and where I could find access to national magazines I railed against the tragic failure of these conferences and against the apathy of our people.

In *The Free World* of July 1943, of the "Diplomatic Mockery" of the Bermuda Conference I said, in part:

"In July, 1938, at the instance of President Roosevelt, representatives of thirty-two nations met at Evian, France, to study the plight of refugees and potential refugees from nazi tyranny. . . .

"The transactions of the Conference were a tragic commentary on political maneuvers. The thirty-two countries had sent their representatives presumably to work out a definite program of relief and to offer asylum to the desperate thou-

87

sands of victims. Yet delegate after delegate rose to announce his country's desire to help and its inability to do so. One declared his country could not receive the refugees because it wished to retain its homogeneity; another communicated his fears of a domestically augmented unemployment problem; another expressed the danger of unassimilated portions infecting the social structure of the country; still another talked glibly of unfavorable climatic conditions. The Conference did not even have the dignity of announcing its failure; it merely fizzled out.

"Enormous graves can be dug and filled in five years."

They were.

Of the Bermuda Conference held five years later in 1943, and to which I addressed myself in the same article, I wrote:

> . . . The results of the Bermuda Conference are a diplomatic mockery of these compassionate sentiments and a betrayal of human instincts and ideals. I do not measure my words because the hangmen of Europe do not tarry.

In a radio address over the Blue Network station, in May 1943, I said:

"The Bermuda Conference has adjourned, but the problem has not adjourned. It cries for immediate solution and not for excuses. There are twenty-eight nations fighting Hitler and yet not one, including England and the United States, has said, 'We will take Hitler's victims.' "

There weren't enough who cared. But there were informed and articulate groups who worked quietly against this public indifference by direct urging to President Roosevelt. By 1944 there were in existence the Intergovernmental Committee on Refugees, the United Nations Relief and Rehabilitation Administration, and, by executive order on January 22, 1944, the War Refugee Board was established for the rescue and relief of war refugees.

It is difficult to describe the sense of helplessness and frustration which seized one when streams of letters poured in from constituents asking help for a sister, brother, mother, child caught up in the Nazi terror. There is one day which is marked out from all others during this period. It was a Tuesday. I can't say how I remember it was a Tuesday—I just seem to remember it that way. Into my office came an old rabbi. I never grasped his name, but everything else about him, his hat which he didn't remove, his long black coat and patriarchal beard, the veined hands clutching a cane, these stand before me, even to this day. Trembling and enfeebled, he had travelled from Brooklyn to Washington to talk to his Congressman. Not once did he seem conscious of his tears as he pleaded. "Don't you see; can't you see; won't you see that there are millions—millions—being killed? Can't we save some of them? Can't you, Mr. Congressman, do something?"

"Do something!" I had talked and written to President Roosevelt. He replied to me:

THE WHITE HOUSE

WASHINGTON

October 21, 1942

My dear Mr. Celler:

You have raised a question in your letter that for some time has given me deep cause for thought. The end we have in view is identical and there only remains a question as to how best we can relieve the persecutions and sufferings of these unhappy refugees in unoccupied France, many of whom have already been returned to the hands of those human butchers in central Europe from whom they believed they had successfully escaped.

Shortly after Mr. Laval came to power last spring I withdrew the American Ambassador from Vichy and left in charge of our interests there a United States Government official who, under instructions from this Government, has recently made strong and repeated protests against the inhumane attitude of Premier Laval towards these refugees. Our representative also stressed the fact that the world, and the people of France, would one day pass judgment on Laval for this callous act. Likewise, only a few days ago our own Secretary of State sent for the French Ambassador in Washington and in no uncertain terms impressed upon him the views of this Government. Under the circumstances there is no possible question but that our attitude is very fully known.

Unfortunately we have to face the disagreeable fact that most of the damage has already been done and, as a practical matter, we have considered that the wise course now is to concentrate on assisting those refugees who remain, and who already had permission to enter other countries, to obtain exit permits from the French Government and make their way to neutral ports. We are also concentrating on a program of assembling and caring for as many children of these refugees as possible, many of whom, as you know, are to come to this country. Permission for the departure of these children from France was only recently obtained by our Charge d'Affaires at Vichy after protracted negotiations with Premier Laval, and even now all of those whom we would wish to help have not been permitted to depart. In the meantime, the American Red Cross is distributing milk in so far as possible among the needy children in unoccupied France regardless of nationality.

These are the positive actions which we are pursuing as diligently as we can.

Although the powerful and moving appeals which you enumerate in your letter have apparently been made in vain, I shall not overlook your further suggestions. I cannot ignore the very real danger, however, that any further statement giving true expression to American feelings on the subject might imperil the admittedly limited but useful program which we have succeeded in working out with Vichy.

Very sincerely yours,

/s/ Franklin D. Roosevelt

The Honorable
 Emanuel Celler,
  House of Representatives.

I had talked to officialdom. "We cannot," I was told, "divert shipping for the transportation of war materials and troops for the refugees, and if we could, how could we reach them? How could they get to us? How could we get to them?" "We will try, of course," I had been told. I tried to tell this to the old rabbi. I tried to tell him, too, that I was convinced that these officials of the State and Treasury Department wanted to do something. I believed this. But the rabbi kept interrupting, striking his cane on the floor of the office. "If six million cattle had been slaughtered," he cried, "there would have been greater interest. A way would have been found." "These are people," he said. "People."

I dreamed about him that night. The old rabbi stood on a rock in the ocean, and hordes of people fought through the water to get to that rock. And the people turned into cattle and back again to people. I was on shore, held by a rope which somebody was pulling back.

What was the answer? The next morning, with the quietness that comes only with conviction, I, for myself, found a partial answer for these people—Palestine. Intellectually, for many years now, I had approved of a national homeland for the Jews in Palestine. But this day the heart was caught and held captive by that ideal. I will come back to this subject later.

The many of us who worked on the Displaced Persons question knew that this was no complex problem. In fact, it was and still is, of all the knotty problems which face us, the easiest of solution. Let countries open their doors, each to the extent of its absorptive capacity, and the problem could dissipate itself in quick and orderly fashion. We needed only to arouse public support and receptivity. That work began, at first quietly and then in an accelerated, mounting crescendo. The accumulated weight of public utterances, radio programs, editorials wore down public resistance until, by 1947, over ninety national organizations representing some forty million people, Displaced Persons Committees in more than fifty cities, and eighty newspapers published in sixty different cities in twenty-five different states joined forces to attain the enactment of Displaced Persons legislation.

In 1947, during the Eightieth Congress, Mr. Stratton of Illinois introduced a bill to admit 400,000 displaced persons into the United States at the rate of 100,000 per year. With the possible exception of the prohibition issue, I believe that more mail was received on this proposed legislation than any other that had been offered since I came to Congress. Thousands of petitions were filed; telegrams, memoranda, and pamphlets crowded the Congressional desks. Ten days of hearings were held. I was a member of the subcommittee which heard the testimony.

As I write this now, a curious fact emerges. All my life, in one way or another, I had been involved and associated with the immigrant and with the facets of immigration and naturalization. I had grown up with the story of my grandparents' flight to freedom from Germany to America in 1848. I was born in and lived in an area of immigrants and the children of immigrants. I had worked my way through law school selling wine to Italian immigrants, who later became my first law clients. In Congress I had become identified with the subject. One of my most successful endeavors in the Congress had been the enactment into law of the legislation sponsored by Clare Booth Luce and myself to give the people of India an immigration quota allotment, where before they had been racially ineligible. This is a good story; I shall tell it later.

In 1946 the Legislative Reorganization Act placed the subject matter of immigration and naturalization within the jurisdiction of the Committee on the Judiciary, of which I was then ranking Democratic member. Heretofore, it had been a separate standing committee. Now, for the first time, I was, through no act of my own, in a pivotal spot in relation to immigration. It almost seems eerie, like the slow emergence of a foredestined pattern.

I remember those meetings of the subcommittee which followed the hearings. I remember how we fought behind closed doors. There were those who resisted bitterly the enactment of any Displaced Persons legislation and there were those who, though opposed to such legislation, knew that the public demanded that this problem be faced and that this clamor must be met some way. There were six members on that subcommittee, of a membership of twenty-six of the full committee. There were those who, knowing the almost fanatical opposition of Senator Revercomb of West Virginia to such legislation and knowing that he was in control of this legislation in the Senate Judiciary Committee, argued for a compromise bill. "Better," they said, "half a loaf than none."

These differences had to be resolved. It was finally decided not to report to the full committee the Stratton bill but to write another bill, cutting the number in half, admitting 100,000 each year, charging their admission against the quotas of the countries of their birth, and obtaining assurances that they would not become public charges, as well as giving preferences to certain types of skilled labor.

The compromise bill was submitted to the full committee and was accepted. The Stratton bill was tabled. The same arguments for and against were heard in full committee: "We want none"; "we want all"; "we want some." The same arguments came up again on the floor of the House. To get anything at all was like pulling teeth without anaesthesia.

The compromise bill passed the House. So it went over to the Senate Judiciary Committee, and in the controlling hands of Senator Revercomb it was ripped apart. When it finally emerged from the Senate Judiciary Committee it wasn't "half a loaf"; it wasn't even half a slice. The number was set at 220,000 displaced persons. Special priority was given to displaced persons of the Baltic States. Only those for whom camp records existed as of December 22, 1945 could be deemed eligible. This was aimed at excluding the Jews and the Catholics, who were not able to get into the Displaced Persons Camps established in Germany and Austria until 1946 and 1947. Forty per cent of the 220,000 were to be allotted to the Baltic States and Poland east of the Curzon Line. In other words, forty per cent of the visas had to be withheld from all other groups, no matter how many there were who were otherwise eligible. Another thirty per cent preference was given to those who were primarily agriculturists, which meant again a search for persons qualified to meet this preference. For the first time in the history of immigration legislation, the legislation demanded that before these people could enter, there must be both housing and jobs waiting. Visas were charged to future quotas, tying up small-quota countries to the extent of fifty per cent for many as much as a hundred years. Only those who were actually in Displaced Persons Camps could be deemed eligible, although many, many displaced persons outside of the camps were fighting valiantly to make their way. In short, it was a discriminatory, unworkable bill. It was, at best, a small gesture aimed to satisfy the pressure of public opinion.

It passed the Senate. The House and Senate Conferees met to work out the differences between the version which had passed the House and the one which had passed the Senate. As one of the conferees, I refused to sign the conference report. I could not in all conscience accept it and believe that it solved anything in any way. The conference report was brought to the floor of both Houses and passed. We had lost another fight for the people.

In 1948, because of the Democratic victory at the polls in November, I became Chairman of the Committee on the Judiciary. One of the first things I did was to introduce the act to amend the Displaced Persons Act of 1948. This time public opinion was not to be disregarded. I will not go through again the fight in the committee, the fight on the floor, the fight in the Senate Committee and on the Senate floor and the conference. I wish only to state that again and again I had to declaim that after one-fourth of the life of the Act had expired—an act calling for the admission of 220,-000 people—only 2,499 displaced persons had been able to gain entry.

This time we succeeded. The cut-off date was moved forward to January 1, 1949, wiping out discrimination against Catholics and Jews. We eliminated the statutory preferences of thirty per cent and forty per cent given to agricultural workers and to the Baltic countries. We increased by 2,000 the number of orphans to be admitted as non-quota immigrants and raised the total number of persons to be admitted from

220,000 to 339,000. The Celler bill became Public Law 774 on June 25, 1948.

Again, this was not the work of one or of many. Behind all of us was the solid, inescapable fact of public acceptance. Perhaps the time will come when the public will be brought to the examination of the national origins theory imbedded in our immigration law, and when that times comes this denial of democracy will be erased.

When the recent bill was enacted by the Eighty-second Congress, revising our Immigration and Nationality Law—a bill which was vetoed by the President as discriminatory and passed over his veto—the Congress retained the national origins theory. But I noted in the debate on the floor that no longer did the members of the House or the Senate rise in hate to attack aliens as they did some twenty-eight years ago. They no longer had behind them such public indulgence. If the reasons for retaining the restrictive immigration policy were no different, the phrasing most certainly was. The alien mixtures in our blood are too widespread now to permit such license as was indulged in in 1924.

Let it not be thought that clear heads and steady pulses prevailed throughout the arguments, the debates, the conferences, which culminated in the enactment of the bill. Friendships were broken; enmities incurred. Antagonisms flourished. The opponents of the bill had thrown themselves into battle with the ferocity of a mother protecting her young. Privately accusations were hurled about, which only the passions of the moment could excuse.

Strategy was discussed, decided upon, and discarded; new strategy devised. Those opposed to the bill believed, and with good cause, that the year 1952 did not augur well for the passage of liberal immigration legislation. They were determined that such legislation should not pass. Equally determined were the proponents of the legislation. It was evident from the beginning that the contending forces were unequally matched. Those who opposed the legislation were, in the main, private citizens and organizations, with a small number of Congressmen from industrial areas on their side. The proponents of the legislation, in the main, were the members of Congress. The outcome was clear from the beginning.

Early in the Eighty-second Congress a House bill and a Senate bill had been introduced, differing in some aspects but, on the whole, using a similar approach to the problems of immigration. The House bill introduced by Representative Walter contained more liberal features than that introduced by Senator McCarran. I introduced a third bill, differing from the two in many vital aspects, in an effort to liberalize the provisions of our immigration laws. The Subcommittees on Immigration of the Senate and House Judiciary Committees proceeded to schedule joint hearings on the two bills only. My bill was not to be included. True, my bill had been introduced later than the other two, and plans had advanced for such joint hearings where it necessitated changing a good deal of the preparations to permit discussion of a third bill, which differed radically. I insisted, however, that my bill be placed on the agenda of the hearing, along with the other two. "Insisted" is a polite word. I literally elbowed my way through.

Twelve days of hearings were held. The subcommittees separated after the hearings, and each proceeded to write a bill. While the Senate subcommittee, in a new bill, inserted liberal changes of minor import, the House subcommittee rewrote a number of provisions, adopting several of the suggestions I had offered in my bill. But the basic restrictionist approach to immigration was not changed.

Since discussions on the bill in the Committee took place in executive session, I cannot reveal the nature of the discussions there. I can say, however, that at the end of each meeting I knew that a really liberal immigration bill, particularly the discarding of the national origins theory, had no more chance of being enacted this session than could a bit of butter remain intact on a hot stove. Every amendment I offered, save two, had been defeated in the Committee meetings. When the bill was reported favorably, in the printed report I stated my own views, as follows:

"The revision of laws presents a unique opportunity to legislators to make good law. Hence, H. R. 5678, revising the laws relating to immigration, naturalization, and nationality merits the most careful scrutiny, because the law therein contained affects basically foreign policy, constitutional guaranties, public welfare, the health, the economy, and the productivity of the Nation. During deliberation of the full committee on H. R. 5678, it became increasingly clear that if we were to make good law, certain provisions could not be deemed acceptable.

"It must be kept in mind that this legislation will have far-reaching consequences, for better or for worse, and I wish to point to those measures which stand glaringly in need of amendment.

"Section 212 (a) provides that the President may *at any time* establish an iron curtain against the entry of any and all foreigners into the United States. Such a delegation of authority constitutes an abdication by Congress of the control of immigration. There is a vast difference between giving such powers to the President in times of declared national emergency or war, which is presently existent, and giving him such powers *at any time*. This is a dangerous substitution of government by law, by government by man. I most strongly urge the retention of present law. I can conceive of no

102

situation which demands that the President be given such powers. [Italics supplied.]

"The Immigration Act of 1924, establishing the annual quotas for countries based on a computation of approximately one-sixth of one per cent, presumably reflects composition of national origin of the inhabitants of the country in the year 1920. Due to the rigidity of our quota system, during the twenty-seven years the present quota law has been in effect, only forty-four per cent of the possible quota immigrants have actually been admitted. Of the total number of 154,-000 annual quotas permitted under the law, 65,700 are allotted to Great Britain; 25,900 to Germany; and 17,800 to Ireland. Every other country having a quota is accorded a quota allotment of less than 7,000. This startling discrimination against central, eastern and southern Europe points out the gap between what we say and what we do. On the one hand we publicly pronounce the equality of all peoples, discarding all racialistic theories; on the other hand, in our immigration laws, we embrace in practice these very theories we abhor and verbally condemn. In the meantime, because Great Britain and Ireland barely use the quota allotment, a large percentage of the 154,000 annual quotas go to waste each year. They are nontransferable. The simple, practical solution—which it seems to me could easily be adopted without even going so far as to disturb the national origin system which is so deeply entrenched (unjustifiably)—would be to take the unused quotas and distribute them among countries with less than 7,000 quota allotments in the same proportion as they bear to the total quota pie.

"It is important that we do so in terms of our own productivity and growth. If we take a long-range view of the position of the United States in the world, we must recognize that our rapid rise to world power during our 176-year history was based upon our population growth from four million to one hundred and fifty million, and this growth was largely the result of immigration. In the years ahead our population is headed for a stable plateau which means an aging population; that is, fewer young persons and more old persons proportionately in the total population. The rate of population growth in the United States is slightly below that required to reproduce itself. The American rate between 1933 and 1939 was 0.96. Compare that with the rate of Russia alone, which was 1.70. The population forecast for the United States in 1970 is 170 million people. The population forecast for Russia alone in 1970 is 251 million. The implications are clear.

"It is also admitted that our supply of unskilled and semiskilled labor is rapidly narrowing as production for defense needs increases. H. R. 5678 retains the rigidity of our quota system. The revision of law, as

I have said before, challenges our sense of responsibility, and it is imperative that we address ourselves to the unshackling of immigration shackles so that, at the very least, the 154,000 allotment can be fully utilized.

"It must be noted that immigration is further restricted by the mortgaging of future quotas by the Displaced Persons Act.

"I point, moreover, to the fact that the 1924 Immigration Act, as amended, sought to adjust immigration to the census of 1920. H. R. 5678 retains the use of the 1920 census upon which to base its quota allotments. If the one-sixth of one per cent computation is to reflect the national composition in terms of national origin, then would it not be more logical to use the 1950 census as a base? It must be remembered, too, that the 1920 census was based on statistics which did not have the benefit of modern statistical analyses. We must bear in mind that many names were Anglicized by persons arriving in this country prior to 1920. The Brodsky's became Brody's, and the Brocci's became Brooks. Thus, many persons were categorized in the English column who more properly belonged in other national groups. Without the benefit of the refined statistical research which we have at hand today, the conclusions were often erroneous. The use of the 1950 census instead of the 1920 census could, again, be easily adopted without making revolutionary changes.

"H. R. 5678 discriminates against emigration from

Jamaica, Trinidad, and other colonies of the British West Indies. Special ceilings within the quotas for the "mother country" are set at one hundred for these colonies, while the natives of all other countries in the Western Hemisphere have nonquota status. Under existing law, natives of colonies or other dependent areas inside and outside the Western Hemisphere are chargeable to the mother country's quota without that new, special restriction.

"Under H. R. 5678, the theory of nativity as the determining factor in the granting of immigration visas is discarded when it comes to persons of oriental stock. The effect in Asia of such discrimination will have far-reaching effect and will supply ammunition for Communist propaganda in that troubled area of the world. H. R. 5678 places a special stigma on oriental or part-oriental ancestry. Although the proposed measure takes a most important step forward by making all people, regardless of race, eligible for immigration, the very same provisions of the bill establish a racial discriminatory rule for admission by declaring that a person born in any European or other country, outside the Asia-Pacific triangle, "who is attributable by as much as one-half of his ancestry to a people or peoples indigenous to the 'Asia-Pacific triangle,' " shall be chargeable—not to the quota of his country of birth —but to the quota of the country of such of his ancestors as were Asiatic, or, if no such quota exists, to the "Asia-Pacific triangle" quota of one hundred. As was stated succinctly by one of the witnesses:

> " 'We are thus, in effect, announcing to the millions of inhabitants of that area that we are continuing arbitrarily to attach an onus to their national identity and that, as far as this country is concerned, they will never escape that onus no matter to what ends of the earth they may migrate.'

"The proposed text would certainly be offensive to the countries of Asia to whom we attribute a contaminating ancestry. Tragic consequences are foreseeable, as a result of such legislation, in the development of our foreign policy vis-à-vis Asia.

"Under H. R. 5678 it is provided most commendably that a former Communist or totalitarian may recognize his mistake and become a useful member of a democratic society, provided his history shows that for five years prior to the application he has departed from these ideologies. This theory of redemption is in keeping with the best ethics of our country. However, the alien resident in this country must show a period of ten years' good behavior before he enters within the circle of those redeemed. Why ten years for the alien in this country and five years for one abroad? If a period of five years is considered sufficient evidence of reform for one, it must be considered sufficient evidence for the other.

"I direct your attention to the provision in section 241 (a) (5) which provides, among other things, that an alien is deportable who has failed to comply with the provisions of the Alien Registration Act of 1940. Those familiar with the procedures of registration can readily see how much mischief can flow from this broad language. An alien who is a permanent resident under the law calls at the post office for a registration address card and must file such card beteen January 1 and 10 of each year. Millions are filed within that same period. Such cards are easily lost, either in transmittal to Washington or through error of the clerk. The alien, for various reasons that arise because of the vagaries of human life itself, may have failed to file such address card with the post-office clerk. Certainly, so harsh a penalty as deportation is far out of proportion with the crime. Such a provision, if harshly administered, can work undue hardship. I believe that the language "reasonably excusable" or "not willful" does not ameliorate the injustice of the provision. Such a penalty is not in keeping with the principles of our jurisprudence.

"Laws should be consistent with our national strength and ideals, and legislation should not be considered through lenses of prejudice and fear. There may be other members who, on considering this legislation, will find areas for improvement which I have failed to mention. So much the better, then, if the members of Congress, working together, supplement each other's work to the end that the best of which Congress is capable is written into law."

I made no friends with this report. It pleased neither those opposed to the bill nor those in favor of it. I was not sufficiently denunciatory, I was told; I had surrendered to the forces of reaction. To breathe, perhaps, that the bill contained some highly desirable provisions was heresy. Among the desirable features of the bill was the elimination of all discrimination against women in our immigration laws (and there had been many such). Another such feature was the elimination for the first time of all racial bars to naturalization, though not to entry. Still another was the enlargement of the non-quota immigrants to include wives, husbands, and children under twenty-one years of age of American citizens. Important in the bill was the use of the "redemption" philosophy, which was, in effect, a liberalization of the McCarran Internal Security Act of 1950. This provision permitted aliens to enter who had abandoned the totalitarian ideology for five years; for the alien resident, however, the period of redemption was extended (unfairly) to ten years. (Under the McCarran Act, once a totalitarian, always a totalitarian, and hence barred from entry, or, if resident in this country, subject to deportation at any time.)

For a brief moment I was startled and even heartsick over the storm that had broken on my head. I felt that for almost three decades I had fought the good fight for liberal immigration and that all these years had been forgotten. I had studied this bill and saw it, as I saw all legislation—the good with the bad. If the bad outweighed the good, does it mean that the good does not exist at all? Would I be honest otherwise?

But when the winds had calmed a bit, more of my perspective returned. How could I expect calmness and appraisal on the part of the opponents when the bill retained the national origin theory and had not made a single change in its structure? Since 1921 liberals had pounded and pounded to remove this blot, this ugly blot. Here was the most appropriate of opportunities, in the revision of the law, to erase the stain, and it had not been taken. What they could not know, nor could they be expected to know, was how adamant were the majorities of the Committees of both the Senate and the House to retain the bars against immigration from Central and Southern Europe. They could not know until they had hit their heads against the unyielding wall, as I had hit mine in the secret executive sessions. They could not possibly know, as I knew, what subsequently the voting on

110

the bill on the floor of both Chambers would reveal. It passed the House by a vote of 206 yeas, 68 nays. It passed the Senate by an overwhelming majority. When the President vetoed the bill, the House overrode the President by a vote of 278 yeas to 113 nays, and the Senate by a vote of 57 yeas to 26 nays.

I am not without hope. As we become more irrevocably tied to the principles of internationalism, we shall more readily understand how integral a part of that commitment is a liberal immigration policy. That change is already foreshadowed by the fact that in the past four years, since immigration was placed under the jurisdiction of the Committee on the Judiciary of the House and Senate, 29,050 persons were by private legislation (including concurrent resolutions) permitted to enter and remain in the United States, who otherwise could not have entered and remained. In the 1952 campaign for the Presidency, both parties promised to work for such liberalization.

I am tempted at this point to indulge in a little aside. At the time the Immigration and Nationality Bill was before the full Committee on the Judiciary, as I said, I offered to the Committee amendment after amendment in an attempt to attain a more just, liberal, and less discriminatory bill. During the course of these amendments, Mr. Keating of New York, Republican member of the Committee, asked that we consider his resolution to set up a subcommittee in the

111

Judiciary to investigate the Office of the Attorney General and the Department of Justice. Because we had held a number of sessions already on the Immigration Bill, it was his opinion, as well as the opinion of others, that we could interrupt these proceedings to consider his resolution. As Chairman I took and held the position that discussion on this bill could not be interrupted. At that time perhaps one or two more sessions could have completed consideration of the measure. The following day I found myself under attack rear, front, left, and right. One-half of the attack centered on the accusation that I was impeding the investigation of corruption in government, and the other half centered its attack on the allegation that I was rushing consideration of the Immigration Bill and aiding and abetting the enemies of liberal immigration legislation.

Truly, a Congressman's lot is not a happy one.

Chapter Seven

It is not a lucky word, this impossible;
no good comes of those that have it
often in their mouth.
  —Thomas Carlyle: *The French
  Revolution*

To turn my thoughts now from immigration to Israel
is to walk from one house to another on the same
street. What was this drive to ally myself with those,
Jew and non-Jew, who fought for the establishment
of a national homeland for the Jews in Israel? It could
not be that the words of a rabbi, poignant and piercing
as they were, could have turned me overnight from
one who thought the Jewish State was a good idea to
one passionately dedicated.

The Nazi terrors had brought many Johnny-come-
latelies into the Zionist fold. I suppose I could be
counted among those. The reasons were of compelling
force. No country would take the Jews. There was the
historic association of the Jews with Palestine for two
thousand years. There were the Jews already in Pales-

113

tine who, since before the turn of the century, were draining the marshes, reviving the tired, wasted soil building for the day of statehood. There was the virus of anti-Semitism which no country in the world had yet succeeded in eradicating. The insistent extolling of tolerance as a virtue reveals the pose of condescension.

That the Zionist conclusions were reasonable and valid I could not and did not doubt. I had believed this at the age of twenty-five when I first read Theodore Herzl's *The Jewish State*. But why, now, this emotional domination by an idea into which for a decade I was to pour my energies, my restlessness and my drives?

I had never thought to define for myself my Jewishness. It was as much a fact with me as the physical fact that my eyes are blue. In my home, when I was a child, there was a naturalness about religion. A benign, personal God watched over us and meted out rewards and punishments in accordance with conduct. We practiced Reform Judaism, which both my mother and father interpreted as the rational approach. Religion was a communal rather than a metaphysical experience.

The voice, the dress, the beard of the rabbi had driven me to remember what I had long ago forgotten. In the calm, taken-for-granted, well-ordered religious practices of my family, I had felt myself denied the turbulence and the vitality and the color of the faith. The way the old women in their voluminous long skirts sat on barrels next to their pushcarts selling sweet potatoes and jelly apples spelled to me the tragedy of the dispossessed. Yet, I felt, they belonged, as did the old Jews sitting on the benches of Tomkins Park, arguing about the *Schule* (synagogue) and the *chazin* (cantor) and the *alte heim* (old country). I knew only a few, scattered words of Yiddish and none of Hebrew, but the texture of their sound I heard in the subways and on the corners of Brooklyn accented my exclusion from the voluble, excitable stream of life and religion. One was the other, and the two could not be boxed apart.

This, as I see it now, motivated my Zionism.

I believe that if all the speeches I made on Palestine and Israel after that day were pieced together you'd have a ribbon to encircle the globe. As a Congressman I had a forum not accessible to older Zionists. I had the floor of the House of Representatives. At all convenient (and otherwise) moments, "Zionist Celler," as *Time Magazine* was to name me, took the floor to plead for United States support for the establishment of a Jewish State.

If I am giving the impression of a lone "voice in the wilderness," let me erase it. The pro-Israel group in the House and the Senate, which included Jew and Christian alike, was vocal and alive to seize every opportunity for the advocacy of their position. Since 1922, when the Sixty-seventh Congress passed its first resolution "that the United States of America favors the establishment in Palestine of a national home for the Jewish people," there had been an increasing interest in the realization of that ancient vision—the Ingathering of the Exiles. The sincere and growing absorption in this theme of the majority of the Members in the House and the Senate added to the cumulative weight of world opinion which, through the action of the United Nations on November 29, 1947, sanctioned the establishment of a Jewish State in Palestine.

But this can only be the story of one man's absorption. No ten such stories, no ten books can unfold fully the drama of the beginnings of Israel.

A passion had seized me. At times I felt like the Ancient Mariner who held his audience captive until he had told his tale. I was a man shaken with fury when on the radio, the floor of the House, and at public meetings I railed against the British White Paper of 1939 which reduced Jewish immigration into Palestine to 15,000 a year for five years at the height of their tragic need. My admiration (besprinkled with awe) for Anglo-Saxon jurisprudence, its culture, its home democracy, its literature, fell below sight as I reviewed its colonial misrule and domination in India, Palestine, and Ireland. Boatloads of fleeing refugees in shaky vessels had drowned off the coast of Palestine because the British would not let them land, just as Indians had died in riots for freedom, and the Irish had torn themselves apart.

For President Roosevelt and President Truman I had prepared endless memoranda on Palestine, presenting them alone or with Congressional delegations. One day, in 1944, I was received by President Roosevelt who, urbane and smiling, bent toward me with a secret. He told me that in a recent conversation, Churchill had told him that when the war ended, the British would consent to the establishment of a Jewish Homeland in Palestine, and that he was glad. Roosevelt added that Churchill agreed with him that the first step would be to wipe out the British White Paper on Palestine and permit escaping Jews to enter without numerical restriction. I could not, of course, betray this confidence at that time, but wherever I could I asserted that I had special knowledge which led me to believe that Roosevelt would supply the impetus that would open the gates of Palestine to the Jews fleeing from murder. Whether he had so agreed with Churchill I cannot say. Neither was the White Paper abrogated nor did the Conservative or Labor Parties of Great Britain remove the bars.

I know that scarcely a year later, when Roosevelt reported to Congress on his Yalta conferences, he reported likewise his conversations with King Ibn Saud of Saudi Arabia. I listened with dismay and disbelief

117

to his implied repudiation of the Jewish claim to Palestine. After Roosevelt died, Mrs. Roosevelt stated publicly that there never had been such repudiation, that a Jewish homeland in Palestine had been and remained to the end one of his highest hopes. I am sure that Roosevelt instinctively felt deeply for the Jews and their desire for a homeland, but I am also sure that the influences of individuals in the State and War Departments had impeded any action Roosevelt might have wished to take in that direction.

I recall, too, how a handful of Congressmen and Senators went to see President Truman, shortly after he had taken the oath of office, to plead for his open support. Since I had been appointed spokesman, I started to read the joint statement prepared for him. I had scarcely read four sentences when he stopped me. His voice and face were cold as he said, in effect, that he was tired of delegations visiting him for the benefit of the Poles, of the Italians, of the Greeks. I remember his saying, "Doesn't anyone want something for the Americans?" Yet it was the indignant prodding of President Truman which led to the formation in 1946 of the Anglo-American Committee of Inquiry which met in Washington, London, Germany, Egypt, Lebanon, Syria, and Israel to explore once again the question of the Jewish Homeland. It was President Truman who had urged Great Britain to permit 100,-000 Jews to enter Palestine. While that Committee reused to recommend beyond that, it did join in strongly urging the admission of 100,000. It was President Truman who gave the full weight of his office to the support of the United Nations Resolution recommending through partition the establishment of a Jewish State. It was President Truman who gave *de facto* recognition to Israel on the very day, May 14, 1948, Israel declared its independence and its statehood.

So I look from face to face and ask myself, "How's guy to know?" Roosevelt's was the word and Truman's, the deed.

In retrospect, it seems that each week brought a new crisis. Early in 1944, the Committee on Foreign Affairs, with the late Sol Bloom as Chairman, held hearings on a House Resolution which read:

> Whereas the Sixty-seventh Congress of the United States on June 30, 1922, unanimously resolved 'that the United States of America favors the establishment in Palestine of a national home for the Jewish people, it being clearly understood that nothing shall be done which may prejudice the civil and religious rights of Christian and all other non-Jewish communities in Palestine shall be adequately protected'; and
>
> Whereas the ruthless persecution of the Jewish people in Europe has clearly demonstrated the need for a Jewish homeland as a haven for the

large numbers who have become homeless as a result of this persecution: Therefore be it

Resolved, That the United States shall use its good offices and take appropriate measures to the end that the doors of Palestine shall be opened for free entry of Jews into that country, and that there shall be full opportunity for colonization, so that the Jewish people may ultimately reconstitute Palestine as a free and democratic Jewish commonwealth.

The public testimony was impressive. What was said in executive (closed) hearing by State Department representatives we never knew. We could only conclude it was not favorable. Key officials, fearing the dynamics of an idea, wished fervently not to disturb the *status quo* in the Middle East, not to offend the Arab princes, or the oil-rich Ibn Saud, not to have to match their wits with the suavity of the British career civil servant—all of which would follow in the wake of a favorable enactment of the resolution.

When the resolution was finally reported out favorably by the Foreign Affairs Committee, we were understandably jubilant. A question in our minds remained, however: Should the resolution fail of passage on the floor, would it not do more damage to the case for the Jewish Homeland than if one had not been considered at all?

120

On December 20, 1945, the House, by overwhelming favorable vote, passed the resolution. It was important, urgently important, for American public opinion to express itself favorably. The resolution effected nothing concretely, of course, but the forceful extension of American approval was another clearing in the forest.

I had followed the floundering proceedings of the Anglo-American Committee of Inquiry with the usual exasperated impatience of the convinced who never understands why the next one doesn't see it as clearly as he does. I was literally in a frenzy of Zionist activity. I travelled to Chicago, California, Minnesota, Florida, Pennsylvania, to make Zionist speeches. I had written to Churchill and to Attlee. And when the wrathful Bevin, British Labor Minister for Foreign Affairs, became the open enemy of a Jewish State, I felt it was a betrayal not to be borne. I knew I was permitting myself the luxury of personalizing a question that transcended personalities.

In November of 1947, after Britain had submitted the question to the United Nations, the United Nations had set up yet another Review Board (the United Nations Special Committee on Palestine). In New York I attended the sessions of the General Assembly debating the recommendations of that Committee. I could not be content with newspaper accounts. When the vote was taken on the majority report, which recommended partition of Palestine, thereby paving the way for a Jewish State as well as an Arab State, the tension around me matched my own. The vote was 33 in favor, 13 opposed, 1 abstaining, and 1 absent. Another crisis had been safely passed.

On May 14, 1948, Israel declared its statehood. That announcement was like the effect of a cannon ball shot into a quiet morning. A call from Eliahu Epstein (later Hebrew-ized to Elath), then representative of the Jewish Agency for Palestine in Washington—later to become Israel's first Ambassador to the United States —brought me to 2210 Massachusetts Avenue, the offices of the Jewish Agency. It was four o'clock in the afternoon. The rooms in the house and the grounds around it were filled with men, women, and children. There was emotion there so thick that you could squeeze it into any shape you wished.

I remember shaking hands with Congressman Sol Bloom and saying, "Isn't it wonderful!" I said to Congressman Javits, "Isn't it wonderful!" I repeated to Eliahu, "Isn't it wonderful!" I said it again to Zahava, Mr. Epstein's wife. All around me people were saying the same thing—"Isn't it wonderful!"

To the crowd Eliahu announced, "We are going to raise the Jewish flag." Everybody walked outside, stood quietly, and turned their eyes upward. As Rabbi Green intoned an ancient prayer, two children raised the blue and white flag of Israel over the building.

Some cried. As the flag reached the top of the mast, the people without signal sang *Hatikvah,* the Jewish national anthem, which had found no home until this day. And when the singing ended, a huge circle was formed in the street and the people in the circle danced the Hora. It is a dance, native to Israel, danced in a circle, hands swinging together in an accented beat at increasing tempo until it becomes a whirl of people in an expression of near-ecstasy.

There wasn't enough room to hold all the people, and we literally crushed our way through the noise and the tears and the talking and the embracing. We suddenly heard Eliahu Epstein exclaim, "Listen, everybody. Listen. I have just received a call from the White House. President Truman has announced his recognition of the State of Israel." If we had felt a moment before that our excitement could rise no higher, we were mistaken. The State of Israel was recognized by the United States. The return to Israel after two thousand years had begun. This was the day.

That night seven Arab nations attacked the day-old little State of Israel.

In October of 1948 Stella and I left for Israel. We were traveling to a little land of some eight thousand square miles, with a population of some 650,000, situated in a hostile Arab world, the latter extending from the Atlantic to the Indian Ocean, an area of some four

123

hundred million square miles, with a population of about seventy million.

By this time I was well versed in the physical facts of Israel. I knew that it was poor in natural resources after centuries of abuse; that land was scarce; that it lacked coal and iron; and that its water power resources were limited. Oil was reputed to be present in the Negev. It had a little bit of manganese, copper, and mica, and the Dead Sea had large amounts of potash and chlorides. Its large industries were the growing of citrus fruits, diamond cutting, chemical industry, some leather production, and so on.

I did not go to Israel to learn about these things. Such facts can be gathered out of Commission and government reports, from propaganda bureaus, and the like. I didn't go to "find out" anything, nor to "see for myself." I went because, until I did, I knew I would still feel perched on the outside rim.

We flew across and landed at the Haifa Airport on a Friday evening, the Sabbath eve. It seems that almost the first thing my eyes rested on were the rude signs printed in Hebrew. It was the first shock of realization that this is the Jewish State. I could not read them, and the old feeling of my childhood crept back over me, the feeling of belonging and yet apart.

Tel-Aviv, Jaffa, Mount Carmel, Haifa, Jerusalem, Lake Galilee, the Negev, the Hills of Judea were names I had repeated for some ten years now—my

124

household words, so to speak. The sighting of these places did not move me. In this I felt the same lack of response to place I had always found before. In Geneva, Paris, London, Frankfort, the façade of a building or the outlines of a landscape failed, some-how, to stir my imagination. Whatever this deficiency, if a deficiency it be, my excitements and responses seem always to be in terms of people. True, there was a magic in the place names of Israel because they be-spoke the continuity of life, the endless weaving of a tapestry whose strands, after two thousand years of dispersion, had reappeared. This I could have glimpsed through my reading—the pageantry of an ancient civi-lization, covered up by the dust of the centuries, and then the re-peopling of the cities and the plains. This did not have to be seen to be understood.

What had to be seen to be understood, at least for me, were the people, the ferment of ideas, the experi-menting, the sense of individual participation in the making of the whole. How can I explain it? Here was a nation, just born, at war with an enemy seven times its size; a nation which was fighting off the enemy with its pioneer-soldiers. In six months it already had an executive, a legislature and a judiciary in operation; customs officials, public health officials, camps to re-ceive the thousands of immigrants pouring in, a sym-phony orchestra, an opera company, theater compa-nies, art exhibits, a university, hospitals, vocational schools, a system of universal education, housing developments—all brought within the outlines of the State.

It appears that a nation had been living underground and had sprung into life at a given signal. There were lusty political parties. The tractor was important, but so was an idea. There wasn't enough to eat or enough to wear or enough houses to live in. Many of the youth—boys and girls—were being killed in action.

As the thought raced through your mind that Israel could not possibly survive, you knew it would. There was an exultant fervor about the people, about the way they walked, talked; an eagerness and a vitality, without a tinge of self-pity for the burdens they bore. They criticized themselves and each other vociferously. There was wit, and there was humor, and there was, over all, a sense of being glad to be alive and the relishing of each moment of life. There was no such thing as a "menial task," as far as I could see. It was a task. From the woman who wrote the script of the daily radio news report for "The Voice of Israel," to the garbage collector, there was pride in participation. Each day had its reason for living, and each person a reason for living that day. I am not exaggerating. Certainly there must have been exceptions to this feeling, but I did not meet them.

In October of 1948, Jerusalem was beautiful and

sad. House after house bore the marks of the Arab bullets. Gunfire was constantly at play. We had travelled over the Burma Road to reach Jerusalem. This road had been built under the scorching sun, almost with bare hands, so that water, food, and medicine could be brought from Tel-Aviv during the siege of Jerusalem. On the Burma Road I saw the overturned trucks and lorries which had been fired upon and destroyed by the Arabs from the surrounding heights. I heard the incessant shots of the snipers in the streets. But the shops were open, the women walked about with their grocery bags, and children scampered on to school as children do the world over. And I visited one of the front lines, where only a street separated the Jews from the Arabs in the old city.

So many of the political words have become threadbare, I am almost afraid to use them, but I can find no substitute for the word "democracy." This is essentially what I found in Israel—democracy that expressed itself in the freedom of opinions and the diversity of its peoples, coming from all corners of the world, in the multiple political parties, in the quarrels of ideologies. The communal settlements of the Kibbutzim worked out for themselves their own structures. Some were entirely communal, others a mixture of individual endeavor and individual reward, coupled with central marketing and central distribution of the products they raised or built. Other settlements were just the grouping of houses, each acting for itself entirely.

When I returned to Israel in the summer of 1951, to the 650,000 inhabitants had been added 500,000 Jewish immigrants. Some 280,000 had come from Central and Eastern Europe; 200,000 from North Africa, Yemen, and Iraq. Forty-four thousand Jews from Yemen—the entire community—had been brought over to Israel by air, a transfer that took eighteen months to complete. Practically all of Bulgarian and Yugoslavian Jewry were now in Israel. The capital funds, the goods and supplies of Israel could not meet the demands placed upon it by the influx of immigrants, despite the almost miraculous increase in industrial and agricultural development. The war was over and won, but the uneasy armistice did not permit Israel to turn aside from the preoccupation with its defense. Arab hostility remained.

But I felt again, and if possible even more keenly, this welding together of peoples from all corners of the earth. While the elder Yemenites and the Iraqis held fast to their ancient cultural patterns, patterns which had not changed in thousands of years, their young were taking their places. It presented a brilliant kaleidoscope of clashing and merging colors. Oriental, East-, Central-, and Western-European, as well as British and American, ways of life poured their influences into a common stream. Some were held firmly in the grip of rigid Orthodox religion. Others, more numerous and certainly more effective, left the practices of religion to the individual conscience, demanding and, in the main, obtaining a separation of Church and State. Many still clung to the dress of their native lands. A Moroccan Jew, given a bed, crawled under it to sleep. A knife and a fork were deemed weapons, not utensils. Pajamas were not sleeping garments, but holiday attire. After the first few days I stopped counting the number of languages I heard spoken in the streets and cafés of Israel. There was the sound of hammering all day long in the losing race to house the exiled come-home-again.

You could not escape the parallel with the United States. This was the miniature melting pot. The parallel cannot be stretched too far, however. Israel did not offer a vast continent, did not offer a land rich in resources. The fusion in America, a fusion not yet complete, has been stretched over a period of many decades. In Israel the count is in months and not in decades.

What national culture will evolve cannot be foreseen, no leader in Israel could predict. When I talked to Prime Minister David Ben-Gurion, he told me that he hoped in one way the composition of the army could hasten the amalgam. The hostility of the Arab world made it necessary that an army be in readiness, he told me, to defend the nation against attack, but that that army, as a pioneer army, could weld the nation together. Through compulsory military training for the 18-year-olds, men and women, Israelis would receive an intense training in agriculture as well as be given broad general education, with particular emphasis on the knowledge of Hebrew. Each soldier would be trained to command as well as to follow. Through these avenues he hoped the young would receive training they could not otherwise receive and would be schooled in the common objective of equality of opportunity for each individual. Each, in serving his State, he hoped, would learn how best to serve himself in the development of his special skills and talents. In this way the young would learn to respect the differences of others, to be comrades in arms and in peace.

As I listened to Ben-Gurion outline this unique military structure, I thought of the young soldier—apparently attached to the Security Division—who had stopped our car the day before, as we travelled to one of the war zones. Not knowing who the occupants were, he motioned for us to pull over to the side. He approached these strangers with a broad grin below his blonde hair and blue eyes. *"Shalom,"* he said; "May I see your credentials?" *Shalom* is the Hebrew word for "peace" and it is the traditional word of greeting. It is certainly a unique experience for an American to have a policeman stop you with the word "peace." It is the word you hear first when you walk into the little leather goods store or the office of the Prime Minister of Israel.

The short, stocky body of Ben-Gurion and the steel blue of his eyes, looking out directly at you from under the white hair (which looks literally as if it had been shot through with electricity), spell out the man of action. These physical characteristics, plus the terse speech and the economy of gestures, give prominence only to the aspect of leadership and hide successfully the scholar and the linguist.

Meeting with Ben-Gurion again in Israel brought to mind the first time I had met him. It was the end of 1946, I believe. Mr. Ben-Gurion was visiting in Washington, and he came up to see me at my office in the New House Office Building. I remember how he stood halved by a streak of sunlight which poured through the wide window. It was an arresting composition; the shade and light on his face and suit seemed to increase the intensity of his stance and his words.

His tone was sharp. "Don't the American people," he asked, "sympathize with our struggle to free Palestine from British rule?"

"Yes," I said, "I believe they do; but actually it is a passive sympathy."

"But that I don't understand. Can't they see that

131

what we want in Palestine is just what they wanted when they fought the American Revolution?"

I wish I could reproduce the timbre of his voice as he spoke. The frustration that ran through it seemed to hit the very walls of the room. Every American must, his tone said, see it the way he saw it—a country shaking the bars and tugging at the chains of its prison.

I must tell this story; it reveals a Ben-Gurion few have ever seen. My then secretary was waiting for a plane at the National Airport in Washington to take her to New York. Her plane, she was told, could not take off and probably would not arrive in New York less than five hours behind schedule time. At the airport she met Ben-Gurion and a friend of hers likewise waiting for a delayed flight, although their plane would take off sooner than hers. "Look," she said to them, "there is a friend of mine waiting for me at LaGuardia Airport. If you should spy her, tell her that I will be five hours late, but that I will be there," and she described her friend to them. In 1948 this same secretary went with us to Israel. At the official reception accorded us, I took her arm, propelling her forward to meet the Prime Minister. I started to say, "I want you to meet . . ." but before I could finish, he broke into a broad grin and, with his face alight with recognition, quickly said, "You know, I never found your friend." It was only after she told me what had

132

happened two years earlier, leading up to this remark, that the humanity of this man pierced me.

I was profoundly impressed by the fact that the leadership of Israel is to be found in the men who, though notable as men of action, have devoted themselves to a lifetime of special studies. Members of the Knesset (the Parliament) number among themselves the highest percentage of economists, historians, and political scientists to be found in any legislative body in the world, I believe. Chaim Weizmann was noted for his contributions to chemistry. Ben-Gurion is a student of Greek philosophy. Moshe Sharett, Minister of Foreign Affairs, is a master of languages; among them Hebrew, English, Arabic, German, French, Turkish, and Russian. He is, as well, a student of music and music forms. Theirs is a breadth of vision fed by the knowledge of the humanities, the arts, and the sciences.

I saw it again in Walter Eytan, Director General of the Foreign Office. In 1946 he had left his post as don at Oxford University in England. He had come to run the Diplomatic School of the Jewish Agency, the agency which had prepared the machinery of the State before statehood. In 1948, when I met him, Eytan was less than forty years of age. When I told him that it was remarkable that so young a man, comparatively, should occupy this office of tremendous responsibility, he smiled and said, "We are a young country. I am talking in terms of people and not of time. The median age in Israel now is somewhat less than twenty-eight. That our people are so young is the measure of our hope for the future."

When he told me this, I thought of Nachum Stern-berg, the liaison officer of the Foreign Office. Young, brisk, decisive, and even, at times, explosive, it was he who took us in tow and led us through Israel.

Then, there was Esther Herlitz, in her twenties, who was on loan from the Israeli Army and Acting Head of the United States Division in the Foreign Office. It was she who talked to me with a sense of historical continuity, with a wisdom far beyond her years. "Israel," she said, "will be the bridge between the East and the West. The Orient and the Occident will meet with the meeting of Jews from continents which have never touched."

I thought of Riva, the young chambermaid who made our beds and scrubbed our floors in the Hotel Gat Rimon in Tel Aviv. "Do you wish to come to America?" I asked her one morning. "No," she said; "my place is here. I work long hours, I work hard; it is not always pleasant. But here I am needed."

I returned from Israel feeling that for a very short while I had been privileged to touch the raw material of history.

Chapter Eight

> *Oh, it is excellent*
> *To have a giant's strength; but it is*
> *tyrannous*
> *To use it like a giant.*
> —Shakespeare: *Measure for*
> *Measure*

Curiouser and curiouser. As I go through the material
before me of my years of activity in Congress, I am
again struck by the same thought which has occurred
to me before. Those which have been some of my
most absorbing legislative interests—immigration, civil
rights, civil liberties, the study of monopoly and monopoly power—were interests I brought with me to
Congress on the fourth of March, 1923. Among the
nineteen jurisdictions assigned to the Committee on
the Judiciary by act of Congress are immigration, civil
rights, civil liberties, and monopoly. I was not aware
when I started work on this book that this fact would
poke its head through many times over.

From 1923 to 1929 I served on the Committees on

Accounts, Claims, and Civil Service. Of these, the Committee on Claims absorbed me most. It is not difficult to understand why, since the bills in that Committee are private bills of relief for individuals who, though injured, have no recourse through the courts of law or the administrative agencies. Congress is thus the last resort to which the injured person can repair in search of equity and justice. The Committee on Claims was assigned to the Judiciary Committee in 1946.

If I were mystic, I could search for some special meaning in the fact that I became Chairman of the Committee on the Judiciary with the dramatic Democratic victory in 1948. Since I am not mystic, I shall let it stand merely as recorded fact.

I have read many thumbnail sketches of myself. Almost invariably the phrase appears: "Pro-labor, New Dealer, Trustbuster Celler." It has become a wheel of rhythm in my head. On more than one occasion I have been tempted to retort:

> Pro-labor, New Dealer
> Trustbuster Celler—
> A mouthful of moniker
> For an old Brooklyn feller.

I don't. It might disturb the public picture of the grim, determined, hard-hitting Congressman.

I do not say that this public portrait is altogether awry. What is a man's worth without indignations?

I see among the papers spread before me a letter from the Business Advisory Council for the Department of Commerce inviting me to address that group on January 17, 1950. One paragraph reads: "We hope that you will be willing to address the group for about twenty minutes. Chairman Mead of the Federal Trade Commission will be the only other speaker. Representatives of the press will not be present." Pencilled in red in the margin is my note to the Chief Clerk of the Committee: "Say 'Yes,' and prepare my triple-plated armor suit and sharpen my cutlass." I knew I was going forth to battle. The subject was to be monopoly and monopoly power.

As Chairman of the Judiciary Committee I jumped with both feet into the heart of the problem. In January of 1949 I had begun my duties as Chairman, and by July of that year I had a Special Subcommittee working at full blast to study the growth of monopoly power. I had been working steadily toward that center since the Sixty-ninth Congress (1926) when I introduced House Resolution 73, calling for the investigation of the American Telephone and Telegraph Company. In the Seventieth Congress, I introduced H. R. 10087, a bill to prevent obstruction and burdens upon interstate trade and commerce in copyrighted motion-picture films.

137

I introduced House Resolution 158 in the same Seventieth Congress, calling for the appointment of five Members of the House of Representatives to investigate the subject of foreign loans by American bankers. In the Seventy-first Congress I reintroduced the same bill; and in the Seventy-second Congress, again, the same bill. In the Seventy-second Congress I also introduced a bill to strengthen the Federal Trade Commission, and so on through the Congresses.

Perhaps the key to my interest lay in the word "opportunity." It was the word most used at home, and it was the word most used in Boys High School and at Columbia University. It was the word that brought the thousands upon thousands of immigrants from Europe into the United States. Diverse and plural as the United States is, its heterogeneous population is tied together by a shared belief in the future; the child's lot will be better than the father's. This sums up the American dream.

In 1927, for the first time, I travelled through Europe, bringing with me, quite naturally, the American standard of material well-being. I observed what every American traveller, naive and otherwise, took pride in remarking—the differences between European and American tools of living. Making that observation and letting it go at that was not enough. There must be a reason for this difference, for this concentrated wealth in the hands of a few and the grim daily struggle for bread for the majority of the people.

I remember talking to Thomas Masaryk when I was in Czechoslovakia. We talked in his high, wide study lined with books. There were books everywhere. As I walked in, I caught glimpses of the other rooms and every room was overladen with books. His study was the room of a man searching in the books of history, political science, economics and in poetry for the answers for his people, so that political and social democracy could mark the progress of the new Republic of Czechoslovakia. Primarily we talked about his hopes for Czechoslovakia. He was like a man consumed by hunger. If that economic pattern, he told me, of the much for the few and the little for the many could be broken, then that could be the beginning of a new era of hope.

In 1932, and 1948, in 1951 and in 1952, when I again returned to Europe, that problem still remained. In the meantime I had learned much about it. European producers, fearing the waste and the pains and the duplications of competition, had always proceeded on what they considered the rational basis of production. Trusts and international cartels would assure stability of prices, diversity of markets, and stability of output. All production was to be a neat pie, giving so many portions and no more. European production, to keep its profits high and its headaches few, rejected the vigor of competition, the infusion of new ideas, the prod and the spur of matching wits, which create the dynamic economy.

To mark the differences between the European and the American economic opportunities was not to deny that this problem was completely absent in the United States. There was a time when this problem could be dramatized, when the word "monopoly" had so evil a sound that it was never absent from any politician's vocabulary when he sought public favor. In 1890 it had led to the enactment of first the Sherman Anti-Trust Law and again in 1914 to the Clayton Act, aimed to prevent the economic stranglehold of big trusts. Franklin D. Roosevelt remarked in 1944, "The Sherman and Clayton Acts have become as much a part of the American way of life as the due process clause of the Constitution."

I find it is different now. Response to the problems of monopoly and monopoly power seems to have disappeared like the street corner orator. It almost seems to me at times that the interest in monopoly and monopoly power shot forth in one explosion to give us the Sherman and Clayton Acts and then collapsed. There had been a great public washing, and that the clothes might need washing again did not seem to concern most of us. The Sherman and Clayton Acts cover every monopoly situation.

But do they?

Perhaps I would not have been caught up so completely in the problems of monopoly power had I not seen it at work firsthand. Perhaps, yes; perhaps, no; I cannot say. In 1928 I formed the Brooklyn National Bank and acted as Chairman of the Board. It was an independent banking institution which had a capital surplus of over two and one-half million dollars. With the signs of the approaching depression, we decided to sell the bank. We received a satisfactory offer from the Adams Express Bank and Trust Company and made the necessary arrangements for transfer. Just before the consummation of the sale, the Adams Express Bank and Trust Company suddenly withdrew its offer. We then received an offer to buy from the Chatham Phoenix Bank, and again, and just as suddenly Chatham Phoenix Bank withdrew. Two offers and two such sudden withdrawals could not be coincidental. Apparently certain influences were at work. The Manufacturers Trust Company would buy, so we were politely informed. After the two withdrawals, we received no other offers. We were forced by prevailing economic conditions to sell for the protection of our stockholders. I will not go into the terms of the arrangement made with the Manufacturers Trust Company. The stockholders were protected, but so sharp were the terms of the contract which we were compelled to sign that it resulted in the loss to me of a most substantial sum of money. For many years thereafter it took the major portion of my earnings to repay it. I did not, of course, consider insolvency proceedings which could have reduced the debt and injured the creditors.

This to me was not the ultimate in disaster. I had my law practice, and I was a member of Congress. But there were others who could be and had been crushed by the exercise of such power. So I began intensely the exploration of the conditions, the theories, the practices, and the threats of monopoly power.

In 1933 I came across these words of Mr. Justice Brandeis:

> The typical business corporation of the last century, owned by a small group of individuals, managed by their owners, and limited in size by their personal wealth, is being supplanted by huge concerns in which the lives of tens or hundreds of thousands of employees and the property of tens or hundreds of thousands of investors are subjected, through the corporate mechanism, to the control of a few men. Ownership has been separated from control; and this separation has removed many of the checks which formerly operated to curb the misuse of wealth and power. And as ownership of the shares is becoming increasingly dispersed, the power which formerly accompanied ownership is becoming increasingly

concentrated in the hands of a few. The changes thereby wrought in the lives of the workers, of the owners and of the general public are so fundamental and far-reaching as to lead . . . scholars to compare the evolving 'corporate system' with the feudal system; and to lead other men of insight and experience to assert that this 'master institution of civilized life' is committing it to the rule of a plutocracy.

All the familiar symptoms arose—the impatience, the urgency, the fever—that always seize me when I first grasp what appears to me to be an essential truth. Here again was an idea which would give me no rest until I held it up to the light, turned it around, upside down and inside out. The first step was preparation, as it always was. The words of Brandeis had set the exploration into disciplined channels where only generalizations had been before.

The first discovery I made was of a basic defect in our anti-trust laws. While the Clayton Act of 1914 tried to prevent the formation of monopolies by prohibiting a corporation from acquiring capital stock of a competitor, where such acquisition would lessen competition or tend to create a monopoly, it did not preclude the purchase of the assets by competing companies. It was this omission which corporations seized upon.

I wish I could convey the drama which I found in all the statistical material I read and studied. I became so immersed in the study that I could only see the picture of corporations before me as so many octopuses, reaching out to rake in more and more of the lesser fry.

One report revealed that the two hundred largest non-banking corporations owned about one-third of all corporation assets in 1909. By 1928 they owned forty-eight per cent of the total, and by the early thirty's the proportion had increased to fifty-four per cent. Some 2,500 formerly independent manufacturing and mining companies disappeared as a result of mergers and acquisitions.

I found that corporations reached behind to buy up the sources of supply, such as textile manufacturers purchasing cotton fields, or moved forward, with manufacturers of steel producing end products from garbage cans to nails. One dairy company, I found, had plants in all but six of the forty-eight states, having acquired in a twenty-two-year period more than four hundred concerns which processed and distributed fluid milk, cheese, butter, and condensed and evaporated milk. The same company had a total of one-fifth of the nation's ice cream sales. Paper companies had reached back to acquire producers of pulp and to buy up large stands of timber. Automobile manufacturers had bought iron and steel foundries and other suppliers of automobile equipment. The electrical ma-

:hinery industry had taken over firms producing such items as magnesium alloys, wire, and plastic.

I found that one drug company had acquired no less than sixty formerly independent companies, of which thirty-two had been bought since 1940. So diversified were the firms they bought that the drug company now finds itself making BiSoDol, Kolynos, Anacin, Old English Wax, Three-in-One Oil, Clapp's Baby Food, Duff's Baking Mix, G. Washington Coffee, Chef Boy-Ar-Dee Spaghetti Dinner, etc. As an indication of the importance of acquisitions to the company's growth, its own annual report for 1947 pointed out that the companies acquired since December 31, 1935 (and many had been acquired prior to that time), were responsible for more than fifty-nine per cent of the firm's total sales in its most recent year's operation. The business of the corporation is carried on by some fifty companies and divisions producing, in all, approximately five thousand products. In the United States and Canada it has thirty-seven manufacturing plants, thirty-three research and control laboratories and forty-six operational centers. It has twenty-four wholly owned foreign subsidiaries, with principal offices in London, Buenos Aires, Sydney, Auckland, Mexico City, Dublin, Calcutta, and Durban, South Africa.

Distilling companies had moved into the wine industry, acquiring along the way many other types of business, including the tight cooperage business. As

145

owners of the tight cooperage facilities, they were able to purchase white oak used in the manufacture of barrels. In addition to vineyards, they control ranches and have gone into the pharmaceutical and food fields. In my exploration, I noted that Italian-Swiss Colony Winery, whose wines I had once distributed, had been swallowed up by one of the largest distilleries.

In the nineteen-twenties there were 30,000 banks which did business with borrowers and depositors throughout the country. Today there are some 14,500 such banks, a drop of over fifty per cent. Of these 14,500, twenty-five large banks hold more than thirty-four per cent of the loans held by the commercial banks in the country. A few large concerns exercise control over the lifeblood of the capitalist system, its credit facilities. The Manufacturers Trust Company, which I have good reason to remember, has acquired the independent banking offices of countless competitors, including the Equitable Trust Company, Mortgage Corporation of New York, Flatbush National Bank, and Brooklyn Trust Company. Today the Manufacturers Trust Company is the fifth largest bank in the United States, with more than one hundred offices doing business in Greater New York. On the west coast one corporation controls more than fifty per cent of the banking offices in the State of California, more than thirty-six per cent in the State of Oregon, sixty per cent in the State of Nevada.

I noted that over sixty per cent of our industrial acquisitions was by way of the acquisition of assets. For over a quarter of a century, I found, the Federal Trade Commission had recommended that legislation be enacted to plug this loophole, so that a corporation could be precluded from acquiring the assets as well as the stock of a competitor, where such acquisition tended to create a monopoly. From 1945 to 1948 bills were introduced in the House and in the Senate to accomplish this. In the Seventy-ninth and Eightieth Congresses, the House bill was approved by the full Judiciary Committee but could not be lodged out of the House Rules Committee. The Senate approved a bill in the Eighth Congress, but like the House bill it never reached the floor. One of the first bills I introduced as Chairman of the Committee on the Judiciary was a bill for this purpose (numbered in that Congress H. R. 2734), and on December 29, 1950 it was approved by the President and became Public Law 899. The years of searching, of study, of examination had been partially rewarded.

But this public law provided only one approach to a problem which led from the door of the small corner grocery store to the elevators of the warehouses owned by the large grocery chains. When I appointed the subcommittee to study the growth of monopoly power in July 1949, I had assumed that I would receive the widest possible public support. President Truman had written to me:

Dear Mr. Chairman: I was glad to get your letter of June 30 about the special subcommittee you have appointed to undertake a broad inquiry into the antitrust laws.

I am wholeheartedly in favor of your subcommittee's objectives as you have outlined them to me.

Since the end of the war, other matters, both foreign and domestic, have at times appeared to overshadow the monopoly problem, or at least have been the subject of greater public preoccupation. But it is my conviction that year in and year out, there is no more serious problem affecting our country and its free institutions than the distortions and abuses of our economic system which result when unenlightened free enterprise turns to monopoly. I have watched this situation carefully and I have made sure that the agencies in the executive branch with responsibilities in this field have discharged them as effectively as their statutory powers and appropriations would permit. Moreover, I have repeatedly called to the attention of the Congress the need for stronger powers and more active measures with which to wage the never-ending fight against monopoly.

Thus in my State of the Union Message in January 1947, I said:

"The second major policy I desire to lay before you has to do with the growing concentration of economic power and the threat to free competition in private enterprise. In 1941 the Temporary National Economic Committee completed a comprehensive investigation into the workings of the national economy. The committee's study showed that, despite half a century of antitrust law enforcement, one of the gravest threats to our welfare lay in the increasing concentration of power in the hands of a small number of giant organizations.

"During the war, this long-standing tendency toward economic concentration was accelerated. As a consequence, we now find that to a greater extent than ever before, whole industries are dominated by one or a few large organizations which can restrict production in the interest of higher profits and thus reduce employment and purchasing power.

"In an effort to assure full opportunity and free competition to business we will vigorously enforce the antitrust laws. There is much the Congress can do to cooperate and assist in this program.

"To strengthen and enforce the laws that regulate business practices is not enough. Enforcement must be supplemented by positive measures of aid to new enterprises. Government assistance, research programs, and credit powers should be designed and used to promote the growth of new firms and new industries. Assistance to small business is particularly important at this time when thousands of veterans who are potential business and industrial leaders are beginning their careers.

"We should also give special attention to the decentralization of industry and the development of areas that are now under-industrialized."

Again, in my State of the Union Message in January 1948, I told the Congress:

"Growth and vitality in our economy depend on vigorous private enterprise. Free competition is the key to industrial development, full production and employment, fair prices, and an ever improving standard of living. Competition is seriously limited today in many industries by the concentration of economic power and other elements of monopoly. The appropriation of sufficient funds to permit proper enforcement of the present antitrust laws is essential. Beyond that we should go on to strengthen our legislation to protect competition."

In June of that year, I vetoed the Reed-Bulwinkle bill, which authorized certain exemptions from the antitrust laws for interstate carriers. In my veto message, I said:

"I have repeatedly urged upon the Congress the necessity for a vigorous anti-monopoly program. This bill would be inconsistent with such a program."

The Eightieth Congress, however, overrode my veto.

In my State of the Union message this year, I said:

"If our free-enterprise economy is to be strong and healthy we must reinvigorate the forces of competition. We must assure small business the freedom and opportunity to grow and prosper. To this purpose, we should strengthen our anti-trust laws by closing those loopholes that permit monopolistic mergers and consolidations."

I am gratified, therefore, to learn that your sub-committee is undertaking a serious wide-scale study of the anti-trust laws for the purpose of determining in what respects they can be made more effective in preventing monopoly and developing a competitive economy.

I am glad to request the agencies referred to in your letter to cooperate fully with your subcommittee in this work. I enclose a copy of the memorandum which I have sent to the various agency heads on this subject. I have added a few agencies

to the list you furnished because it seemed to m
that your subcommittee might find occasion t
call on them for assistance.

With all good wishes for the success of you
work in this most important field.

Very sincerely yours,

Harry S. Truman

To the Government agencies he forwarded the fol
lowing memorandum:

Chairman Celler, of the House Committee o
the Judiciary, has appointed a special subcommit
tee to undertake a broad inquiry into the anti
trust laws. Mr. Celler has indicated to me that h
and his subcommittee wish to work in the closes
cooperation with the Federal agencies that ar
concerned with the field of this inquiry.

I strongly favor the objectives of the Celler sub
committee. I am hopeful that its work will pro
duce constructive recommendations and results

I therefore request that you and your agenc
give Mr. Celler and his subcommittee the fulles
possible cooperation and assistance, subject onl
to jurisdictional and appropriation limitation.

Harry S. Truman

I was warmed by this wealth of understanding
Surely, the public interest and response must inevi

tably follow. Did not the problems of monopoly and monopoly power concern the boy just out of school searching for career opportunities in business? Didn't it concern the small businessman and the middle-sized businessman who faced the competition of giant corporations who, through massive advertising, could create a demand for their product and their product alone? Didn't it concern the men and women who had been bought out and now worked as salaried managers and clerks where formerly theirs was the pride of independence and growth achieved by their own ingenuity and hard work? Didn't it concern the butcher, the baker, the candlestick maker, who found less and less opportunity to shop around and choose from a myriad of manufacturers with whom to deal? Didn't it concern the laborer whose job opportunities were confined to fewer and fewer corporations, with the labor policy of corporations determined by fewer and fewer men?

I was wrong. No man has ever been more wrong. I had touched the most sensitive nerve of American pride—its bigness in business. The winds raged, the tides rose, and virtually the mountains shook.

From the opening day of the hearings held by this Subcommittee—July 11, 1949—and for months thereafter I was the subject of cartoons and editorials, copy for columnists, and for feature article writers. Celler was destroying the American heritage. Celler was going to chop down all big business into tiny segments and scatter the pieces. Celler was tinkering with the economic machinery and throwing a monkeywrench in the works. If public approval was absent, public interest was there in full dress. I was invited to address the public via radio and television on such programs as Town Hall, the Labor League, Pro and Con, Congressional Cloak Room, Meet the Press. There were articles for *Readers' Digest,* for law reviews. I was interviewed and photographed, and, above all, denounced.

The bigness of business was responsible for the highest earnings and standard of living in the world. The bigness of business meant American efficiency, meant American production, meant food and clothing for widows and children. How did I even dare question bigness in business? How could I ever suggest that the bigness of business should be looked at with a critical eye? I have used the word "bigness" because that became the popular word for the problem. Actually, the subcommittee was probing the aspects of monoply power. We were not questioning that some businesses must be big, such as those manufacturing airplanes, dynamos, or locomotives. We wanted to know whether a corporation could grow so large as to lose enough in efficiency, lose flexibility, and dominate an industry in such a manner as to produce a sickness in our economy. Can one man—the president of a corporation spread across a continent—keep his reins on the business, from control of the purchasing of office supplies to the determination of marketing policies? Does not business bureaucracy establish itself more rigidly than government bureaucracy, since it is not open to the public view as is government with its systems of checks and balances, of administrative and judicial review? We wanted to know what happens with new technological advancement. Is it too massive an operation for a sprawling, conglomerate corporation to re-tool? Is inertia produced by the very weight of its size, and, if so, what happens to the economy of a country as corporations keep growing and growing?

One witness aptly compared the struggle of the individual entrepreneur against the great combinations as: "Every man for himself," said the elephant as he danced amongst the chickens.

The subcommittee began its hearings on the general problem of monopoly power. We heard testimony from government, from political scientists, from economists, from representatives of the Metropolitan Life Insurance Company, from the Army and Navy procurement officers, from Mr. Greenwalt of the du Pont Company, from Eric Johnston (President of the Motion Picture Association of America), from Herman Steinkraus (then President of the United States Chamber of Commerce), from Emil Schram (then President of the New York Stock Exchange), from Mr. Charles E. Wilson of General Electric. There was no need to prove the hugeness of these vested enterprises. Corporations that testified before the subcommittee felt pride in their empires. And why not? It takes a heap of doing to build that high and that wide.

These were good men before us, but they were indignant men, angry that a question had been raised against their empires. It was not that they feared too close a look; it was indignation as to why anybody would want to look at all, when such a profusion of goods and material was pouring forth into the public lap.

Yet there was testimony before us—the 1946 figures released by the Bureau of Internal Revenue—that disclosed that of all corporations reporting, one-fifth of one per cent owned fifty-six per cent of the assets of all of them. Less than two per cent of the corporations earned sixty-one per cent of the net income of all of them. The Department of Commerce reported that out of 452 industries studied, there were forty-six in which four companies controlled more than seventy-five per cent of the total output of each industry, and 150 industries in which the Big Four controlled more than half of the total annual output. Included among such industries are soap, liquor, meat, steel, automobiles, and aluminum.

During the hearings on the United States Steel Corporation, which the subcommittee held following its exploration of the general question of monopoly power

—hearings which took one month and during which testimony was heard from over fifty witnesses—the following colloquy took place:

> *Mr. Celler.* Mr. Fairless, before the Joint Committee on the Economic Report, you stated as follows, and I am in accord with that, "I personally think that no concern should get larger than it can operate efficiently." You stated that, did you not, Mr. Fairless?
>
> *Mr. Fairless.* That is right.
>
> *Mr. Celler.* What should be done? What should we, as members of Congress, do by way of reinforcing the fabric of antitrust laws if there is a corporation which becomes larger than its efficiency requires?
>
> *Mr. Fairless.* Mr. Congressman, my concept of the problem, as you stated, is this: That you do not need to do anything. That the American people, our customers, and the customers of any company that may be in that position will take care of that situation very beautifully. In other words, any corporation, whether it be large or whether it be intermediate in size or small, will fail if it is operated inefficiently.

The company will fail, eh? So what? If the vegetable man closes up his little shop because he has failed, it is

157

the tragedy of an individual, but if an empire topples, it carries thousands down with it in its fall.

The United States Steel Corporation owns at least fifty-one per cent of the high grade ore in the Mesabi region from which most of the iron ore for steel comes. If the United States Steel Corporation were to stop selling iron ore to its competitors, there would be a catastrophic situation in the steel industry. Plants would close, ghost towns would spring up, and thousands of men would look for jobs. I do not think United States Steel will stop selling iron ore. I merely illustrate the power it has.

The U. S. Steel Corporation owns the principal railroad which must be used to transport the iron ore. This railroad must be used by the competitors of the U. S. Steel Corporation. The Steel Corporation makes more from its iron ore and railroad operations than it does from all the rest of its steel-making facilities.

U. S. Steel, not content to make steel alone, has gone into the manufacture of finished and fabricated steel products. Small manufacturers find that they must buy their steel from a steel company which is directly competitive with them. Other steel companies have done likewise, and now these steel companies can exercise the power of life and death over the small fabricators by raising the price of steel and holding down the price of their own manufactured products. The steel companies can catch the small fabricator in a price squeeze and put him out of business. This has happened.

It would take pages to list the products of the steel companies. Mr. Fairless testified that there were thousands. U. S. Steel has eighty-four subsidiaries. It owns sixteen common carrier railroads. It is in the cement-making business. It is in the pre-fabricated housing business. Testimony revealed that it had resisted for many years technological changes such as the introduction of continuous rolling mills, heat treating processes for the production of sheet, and improvements in the manufacture of tin plate. The giant was too big to turn over.

I must note, though not in passing, the double-edged anger of these corporate gentlemen. One edge is reserved for those who dare to as much as examine size in business; the other for the growth in size of government and organized labor. They did not see the relationship which ran from big business, which called into being big labor unions, and which, in turn, related to the size of government.

I have been at this chapter longer than I had planned. I have gone into much greater detail than I had thought was possible in a book of this kind, but there were so many years of work, so many hours of turning the problem over and over in my mind that perhaps I am over-sold and perhaps I am over-selling. Yet, to me, this problem affects us as profoundly as any other one single problem facing us. If we, as yet, do not know the answers, can we not at least ask the questions?

Throughout the hearings on U. S. Steel I studied the Supreme Court's opinion on the case that was tried by the United States against the United States Steel Corporation in 1948, and I kept before me the words of Mr. Justice Douglas, dissenting from the opinion of the Court:

> We have here the problem of bigness. Its lesson should by now have been burned into our memory by Brandeis. *The Curse of Bigness* shows how size can become a menace—both industrial and social. It can be an industrial menace because it creates gross inequalities against existing or putative competitors. It can be a social menace—because of its control of prices. Control of prices in the steel industry is powerful leverage on our economy. For the price of steel determines the price of hundreds of other articles. Our price level determines in large measure whether we have prosperity or depression—an economy of abundance or scarcity. Size in steel should therefore be jealously watched. In final analysis, size in steel is the measure of the power of a handful of men over our economy. That power can be utilized with lightning speed. It can be benign or it can be dangerous. The

philosophy of the Sherman Act is that it should not exist. For all power tends to develop into a government in itself. Power that controls the economy should be in the hands of elected representatives of the people, not in the hands of an industrial oligarchy. Industrial power should be decentralized. It should be scattered into many hands so that the fortunes of the people will not be dependent on the whim or caprice, the political prejudices, the emotional stability of a few self-appointed men. The fact that they are not vicious men but respectable and social minded is irrelevant. That is the philosophy and the command of the Sherman Act. It is founded on a theory of hostility to the concentration in private hands of power so great that only a government of the people should have it.

I had tried to focus public attention on this problem. Perhaps I had succeeded. I do not know. Few words of comfort came my way throughout these hearings. At the heart of it lay the search for more freedom —a freedom that could not exist long without the opportunities of an expanding social democracy. But perhaps I started something, for the hearings sold by the thousands at the Government Printing Office. Additional thousands were distributed by the committee upon requests from industry, economists, universities.

161

I take comfort in the thought that others may continue the search.

From steel, the subcommittee turned next to the study of the newsprint industry, because available newsprint meant a free pass. The newsprint shortage was acute. Britain, Latin America, India, Asia, and the United States felt and are still feeling the shortages of newsprint. The smaller newspapers in the United States mean a diversity of opinion, freely and independently expressed. In the newsprint shortage, the smaller newspapers were forced either to patronize the black market or merge, or disappear.

While we could find no direct evidence of the monopoly situation in Canada, which controlled, along with Scandinavia, most of the newsprint output of the world, we did find a system of identical prices. We found that fear of overproduction since the depression had wedded the newsprint industry in Canada to stable prices, stable profits, and stable levels of production. There was little effort to increase production. We found that while most of these companies were in Canada they were largely controlled by American interests.

We found that monopoly power in the newsprint industry was having serious repercussions on United States publishers. Since 1950 there were three successive increases in the price of newsprint per ton, simultaneously made by all suppliers—the first of six dollars, the second of ten dollars, and the third of ten dollars. And we found that the answer to both newsprint shortages and high prices lay in greater production. The subcommittee accordingly recommended the exploration of the use of hardwood, begasse, and wheat straw in the manufacture of newsprint.

At the prodding of the subcommittee, the National Production Authority, the Department of Agriculture, the Reconstruction Finance Corporation and other government agencies have undertaken a coordinated program, under the leadership of the Department of Commerce, to discover what new materials can be used in the manufacture of newsprint and what encouragement by way of financing can be given.

It was not so easy as it appears in the writing. But to me, during the cold war, no more vital weapon exists than a free and independent press. For the democracies a newsprint shortage is as disastrous as defective ammunition.

While the newsprint hearings lacked the spectacular aspects of the steel hearing that preceded it, I consider those hearings and the results that followed in governmental experimentation and encouragement as one of the most vital accomplishments of the Committee.

Another industry in the grip of a few large and powerful producers is aluminum, and so we held hearings on aluminum. Thousands of small, independent fabricators scattered throughout the nation were dependent for their very livelihood upon only three manufacturers of primary ingot—Kaiser, Reynolds, and Alcoa. Alcoa, the largest of these, had once been adjudged a monopoly by the Courts. Judge Learned Hand, one of the most able judges to preside in an American tribunal, described the monopoly position which Alcoa at one time held as follows:

> Alcoa's size was 'magnified' to make it a 'monopoly'; indeed it has never been anything else; and its size not only offered it an 'opportunity for abuse,' but it 'utilized' its size for 'abuse,' as can easily be shown.

One of the most important problems in the aluminum industry was to assure adequate supplies to the many small businesses dependent upon primary and semi-finished aluminum from which they produced such products as venetian blinds, pots and pans, containers, automotive parts, etc. Because the manufacture of these finished articles was much more profitable than the production of primary aluminum, there was a danger that the "Big Three" aluminum companies might favor their own fabricating subsidiaries over independent aluminum finishers, especially in times of aluminum shortages.

Evidence that this might have occurred comes from the fact that, whereas in 1950 some seventeen thousand independent fabricators of aluminum were doing business in the United States, by 1952 it was reported that only fourteen thousand such fabricators remained. It was therefore important that these small concerns, which formed the basis of a sound competitive system in the aluminum industry, be guaranteed continuing supplies of primary aluminum.

My efforts to assist this small but essential segment of the aluminum industry met with not only the opposition of industry but the lethargy of Government. Attempts to provide for the entry of new competitors in the field of primary manufacture all proved unavailing except for the project of Anaconda Copper Mining Co., itself a giant in the copper industry. My suggestion that the Government enter into long-term commitments with Canada to insure the importation of primary aluminum to small domestic consumers was at first disregarded. Only in recent days, when it was fully realized that it was absolutely essential to our economy that we resort to additional sources for aluminum other than the "Big Three" in this country, did the United States recommend assistance from Canada. The aluminum hearings had borne some fruit.

Then came the baseball inquiry.

Here I must pause and take a deep breath. If I thought storms had broken furiously over my head before, I knew better when these hearings started. Never had such controversy raged. Never had so many columns been filled with torrents of words. Never before had sports editors, sports writers, sports columnists, had this opportunity which had been given them to parade their knowledge under the noses of eleven Congressman. And here again it was "Celler is out to destroy baseball," "Celler interferes with the national pastime." If I had the impudence to examine big business, how much greater was my impudence to examine organized baseball. I discovered I could match the wrath of any one single sports writer against the wrath of Mr. Benjamin Fairless.

The center of the storm was the "reserve clause" in baseball contracts, a clause which binds a player to a club for the rest of his playing days, unless the club sells him or trades him. One magazine ran an article on "Baseball Player Slaves"; another, "No Reserve Clause, No Baseball."

Actually, three bills had been introduced to exempt organized sports from the operations of the antitrust laws, and these bills had come before the Committee on the Judiciary. Organized baseball's monopoly position had not been challenged for decades, and organized baseball presented itself to the committee as a unique opportunity to study antitrust policies as applied to a self-regulated industry. That organized baseball today is "big business" cannot be denied. But here we have the history of cooperation in the operation of a business and competition on the playing field.

The heat subsided when the subcommittee made it clear that it had no intention of proposing any legislation directed at organized baseball. I think this phase of the subcommittee's experience should be entitled: "The Baseball Inquiry, or The Hornets' Nest."

Chapter Nine

> *Liberty lies in the hearts of men and women; when it dies there, no constitution, no law, no court can save it; no constitution, no law, no court can even do much to help it.*
> —Learned Hand: *The Spirit of Liberty*

I am told that in the index of the Committee on Un-American Activities there is a reference to *Celler, Emanuel, M. C.* This is neither startling nor disturbing news. The passion of that committee for collecting names of those who consistently supported the New Deal is not exactly a secret. But what is disturbing was the hesitation—no, stronger than that—the reluctance in me to state publicly that I had been indexed by the Un-American Activities Committee. I knew that in this reluctance I was facing fear.

Previously, in a speech before the Federal Bar Association, I had stated:

"I firmly believe that our greatest—and I emphasize, greatest—internal danger is that of the

paralysis of fear gripping this country. The split
personality we present is hardly conducive to any
feeling of national dignity. On the one hand we
make a great to-do of the strength of our democratic institutions, of our foundation of Government by law, of the development of our industrial, social, and economic power under those
principles, and on the other hand internally we
cringe not before the thought of the impact of an
atom bomb but before the thought of the impact
of ideas. Courage to travel to the moon, yes—as
we seem to be doing—but courage in the market
place of ideas, no. We are surrounded by distrust
—distrust of ourselves, distrust of our Bill of
Rights, distrust of law. In this distrust of the law
to protect us internally, we fashion more laws
which in turn, we again distrust . . . I have talked
with many of my constituents—student, worker,
businessman, housewife—and many of them are
afraid; afraid, not of any spy lurking under a bed,
or in a closet, or in the guise of an instructor
(they do not feel that the Communist ideology is
a passionate-eyed brunette whose charms are irre-
sistible), but they are afraid of being accused of
heresy should they depart from the expression of
any but the most orthodox of opinions. In short
they are afraid to speak their minds."

The one adjective which consistently appeared in the comments I received was "brave." It was a "brave" speech. I had been "brave" to make it. It had never occurred to me that any kind of courage was needed to talk about the preservation of our civil liberties. I have seen other men silenced by this fear lest the suspicion of disloyalty rest on them, and I had marvelled at them. As I write these lines I think I can now understand a little better the nature of that fear.

At the Democratic National Convention of 1952 I spoke before the members of the Committee on Platform and Resolutions. I pleaded that an anti-McCarthyism plank be included in the party platform. "I offer it soberly," I said, "because it is a sobering and fearful thing that this kind of plank in a national party platform has become a necessity." I read the proposed plank to the members:

> The Democratic Party will never desert the freedoms of our people under the guise of pretending to protect them. We pledge to fight the dark and reactionary forces high in the counsels of the Republican Party which have made political capital out of the techniques of character assassination by innuendo and who have adopted the dishonoring and dishonorable concept of guilt by association. We shall wipe out the climate of fear which has led men of good will to avoid freedom

171

of expression and assembly. We pledge ourselves to reinvigorate our fundamental precept that a man is innocent until proven guilty. We believe firmly that Communism internally and externally can and must be fought without resort to the Communist tactics of the suppression of all individual freedom. "It is this respect for the individual and his rights as an individual which compels our abhorrence of Communism. Communism which feeds on aggression, hatred, and the imprisonment of men's minds and souls shall not take root in the United States. To that end we pledge our every resource."

I went on to plead: "Let's name the evil which has called this plank forth, an evil recognizable to every mature mind. It has a name—McCarthyism. Let us not underestimate the width and the depth of the fear blanketing this country because of McCarthyism. Let us not underestimate how many people, both within the Democratic and Republican Parties and the 'independents,' are crying out for leadership to cut out this cancer. Deliberately and calculatedly, McCarthyism has set before itself the task of undermining the faith of the people in their Government. It has undertaken to sow suspicion everywhere, to set friend against friend, and brother against brother. It deals in coercion and in intimidation, tying the hands of citizens

172

and officials with the fear of the smear attack. I have no wish to indulge in histrionics, but I do know that McCarthyism represents a danger in this country we dare not ignore. I say it is a cold hand creeping over our vitals. The fact that the author of McCarthyism was given the distinction of addressing the Republican National Convention strikes terror in the hearts of honest men. Many who have flirted with the idea of voting the Republican ticket have turned away from that ticket because of the acceptance by the Republican Party of McCarthy and McCarthyism.

"Lest you incline to the belief that I exaggerate, let me refresh your recollection. By innuendo, by the piecing together of bits of events out of context and out of history, McCarthy has sought to brand as traitors such public servants as General Marshall, Dean Acheson, and Philip Jessup. This is Senator McCarthy on the *Christian Science Monitor*—and I quote directly the words of McCarthy himself:

> At the time of Gunther Stein's exposure as an important member of the internationally famous Sorge Communist spy ring I thought that Gunther Stein had cleverly deceived the *Christian Science Monitor* when they made him their China correspondent—that they did not know they were hiring a traitor to America to write the news on China for the *Christian Science Monitor's* readers.

173

But now I *began to wonder* as I watched Strout of the *Christian Science Monitor* and Rob Hall of the *Daily Worker* cheek by jowl during the entire hearing and then read the venomous distorted parallel stories which they both wrote.

"If ever there was a classic example of the smear and the innuendo this is it. I turn to another quotation, another perfect, but perfect, McCarthyism. Mind you, these are direct quotations. In speaking of *Time Magazine,* Mr. McCarthy said:

There is nothing personal about my exposing the depth to which this magazine will sink in using deliberate falsehoods to destroy anyone *who is hurting the Communist cause.* [Italics mine.]

"I need not remind you how McCarthy sought to deprecate *Time* by sending to *Time*'s advertisers his opinions of the magazine.

"Among the newspapers he cites as following the Communist Party line will be found the *Milwaukee Journal,* the *Washington Post,* the *St. Louis Post Dispatch,* and the *Portland Oregonian.* Let me quote again:

Some [says McCarthy] who read those papers may at first blush violently, differ with me. However, you need not take my word. Make your own decision. First check the editorial policy which the

Daily Worker consistently follows. Then determine for yourself the extent to which the above papers follow that editorial policy. Do not be deceived, however, by any general condemnation or tossing of pebbles at Communism generally.

"I believe there has been less common knowledge of McCarthyism's attacks upon a free press. Insidiously, it has moved from government officials to private citizens and then to the great free press of our country. I pray you, gentlemen, let us not ignore this. If McCarthyism had not been given the prominence and honor it received by the Republican Party, we could, perhaps, choose to regard it as the unhealthy manifestations of a troubled era in our history. We will serve our country ill if we keep silent on this issue. This is our enemy. Let us name it and let us fight it."

What emerged in the Democratic platform was two calm little sentences which read:

We deplore and condemn smear attacks upon the character and reputations of our federal workers. We will continue our fight against partisan political efforts to discredit the federal service and undermine American principles of justice and fair play.

I suspect fear had a finger in this phrasing. If you are too vigorous in your protest of the smear, you have to face the accusation of a sneaking sympathy for the Communists.

There have been some lonely moments for me in this fight for civil liberties. I recall that one night at a dinner party, on the eve of a scheduled vote to override President Truman's veto of the McCarran Internal Security Act, there was another Congressman besides myself present. The talk that evening centered around the provisions of this bill.

"You cannot vote to override the veto in all conscience," I told Congressman X.

"But I face a fight at home if I vote to sustain the President," he replied. "My opponent will surely make the most of it." Election was six weeks off.

"You can explain your reasons for your vote when you get home," I told him. "You will see how your constituents will stand behind you."

The next day he called me up late in the afternoon and said, "You win; I voted to support the President's veto." He was *not* re-elected.

Perhaps the loneliest moments I experienced in the House were in the running battle with my former colleague, Mr. John Rankin of Mississippi. Here was a curious mixture. More than any other single member of the House, Rankin had led the fight for Rural Electrification. In the days when TVA legislation needed every ounce of support it could get, Rankin defied all the cries of socialism directed against it and defended t with his great command of parliamentary skill. I believe that had he remained on that track he, perhaps, would have ranked with the late Senator George Norris in the extension of power productivity for the people.

Rankin came to the House the same year I did. The prejudices with which he later became identified he brought with him. He became bolder as the years went by and to his theme of white supremacy he added that of anti-Semitism. To listen to his harangues on the floor became, for me, an agony. I had adopted a special technique in replying to Rankin. Instead of rushing forward to ask for recognition from the Speaker as soon as Rankin finished his statement, I deliberately held back. I waited to see if there was one other to make a reply. I did this so that, if at all possible, I could avoid making the subject of white supremacy or anti-Semitism a personal issue between two members of Congress. It was not necessary that I make the reply; it was only necessary that a reply be made. Sometimes as much as a half hour would go by before I rose to speak. Sometimes the exchange was immediate and hot. These debates make for some good reading. A sample or two of these colloquies will most clearly show the emotions with which they were charged.

In the *Congressional Record* of May 22, 1947, appears the following:

Mr. CELLER. Mr. Speaker, yesterday an attack on the floor of the House was made upon Zionism and for that purpose there was quoted a passage from the memoirs of Henry Morgenthau. There is always some quotation to suit every purpose. The gentleman from Mississippi [Mr. Rankin] whose lack of confirmation on Zionism is readily discernible might well know that the son of Henry Morgenthau, Sr., takes quite a different view and he might also know that every President of the United States beginning with Wilson to Truman supported the aims and aspirations of the Jews in Palestine. Certainly, the support of Zionism given by thirty-nine Governors of the respective States of our Union, and by thirty-three of the State legislatures, and by the platforms of the two great parties, carries more authority and weight than a statement by the deceased Mr. Morgenthau or assertions of the gentleman from Mississippi.

The gentleman from Mississippi [Mr. Rankin] likewise inserts an ad which appeared in a New York paper. That was not an ad sponsored or supported by general Zionism. It was the ad of an insurgent group which opposes the central authority of the Jewish Agency of Palestine, the entity established by the mandate for Palestine. In the interest of fairness, the gentleman from Mississippi [Mr. Rankin] might have acquainted himself with these facts before he spoke.

Mr. RANKIN. Mr. Speaker, I might say in the beginning that I know of no man who in my opinion has done the Jews of this country more harm than the gentleman from New York [Mr. Celler]. I was amused, as well as amazed, at his statement a moment ago.

As for Henry Morgenthau, Sr., he was the brains of the family. In fact he was one of the great Jews of this country; and the intelligent Jews, I am sure, will not agree with the statements made by the gentleman from New York [Mr. Celler] concerning him.

Mr. CELLER. Mr. Speaker, a point of order.

The SPEAKER. The gentleman will state it.

Mr. CELLER. Mr. Speaker, I ask that the gentleman's remarks be taken down. He made certain statements which reflect upon my service in this House when he said he thinks there is nobody who has rendered more disservice to the Jews than I.

Mr. RANKIN. I said, had done them more harm by your continuously agitating a policy that gets them into trouble, and which as Henry Morgenthau, Sr., so forcefully denounced.

The SPEAKER. The Clerk will report the words objected to.

179

The Clerk read as follows:

"Mr. RANKIN. Mr. Speaker, I might say in the beginning that I know of no man who in my opinion has done the Jews of this country more harm than the gentleman from New York [Mr. Celler]."

The SPEAKER. The Chair does not think these words reflect upon the gentleman from New York [Mr. Celler]. They are merely an expression of the opinion of the gentleman from Mississippi [Mr. Rankin] and, of course, it does not necessarily mean that that opinion is shared by anyone else. The Chair does not believe the words reflect in an unparliamentary manner upon the gentleman from New York [Mr. Celler].

The gentleman from Mississippi will resume in order.

Mr. Rankin continued to make his statement on the subject of Zionism, and concluded with:

"As between him and the gentleman from New York [Mr. Celler], I will take Henry Morgenthau, Sr., and I feel sure that ninety per cent of the American people would do likewise, if they knew the facts."

I must, of course, quote my good friend, Representative Arthur Klein, who rose at the end of Mr. Rankin's statement to say:

180

"Mr. Speaker, I do not believe the gentleman from New York [Mr. Celler] needs any defense from me or from any other Jew in this country or in the House of Representatives. I believe the House knows, and I want to say to the Members, if there is anybody who can talk about doing harm to the Jews of this country or any other minority groups, the gentleman from Mississippi is well qualified. He is certainly an expert on that subject."

Most often there was none to reply but myself, and these were the lonely moments.

I go back to a day in 1949—May 11, to be specific—when Mr. Rankin, on the Floor of the House, stated:

"I expect to introduce a resolution to have this so-called Anti-defamation League investigated. When we turn the pitiless sunlight of merciless publicity onto that subversive organization, the House will be astounded and the American people will be shocked."

I was furious. I can even now recall the emotion at that moment. I asked permission to address the House. Again my fury propelled me out of bounds:

Mr. CELLER. Mr. Speaker, I canot let the occasion go by without commenting on the canard that the gentleman from Mississippi was guilty of when he called the Anti-defamation League subversive.

Mr. RANKIN. Mr. Speaker, I demand that those words be taken down.

The SPEAKER. The Clerk will report the words objected to.

The Clerk read as follows:

"Mr. CELLER. Mr. Speaker, I cannot let the occasion go by without commenting on the canard that the gentleman from Mississippi was guilty of when he called the Anti-defamation League subversive."

The SPEAKER. The Chair desires to make a statement. There are too many 'left-handed' compliments being passed around this House all the time on both sides.

The word 'canard' to me conveys the idea that a man has told a falsehood. Therefore, if anybody desires to move to strike it from the record—without objection, the word 'canard' will be stricken from the record.

There was no objection.

What happened not a few times after these colloquies was that Rankin would meet me in the Cloak Room of the House, and offer a friendly gesture, as if to say: "There's nothing personal in this, you know,

Celler." I am convinced he believed that. To him these were broad themes, not to be related to people he knew. I have noticed this many times of people in the grip of prejudice against minority groups. The people they know are, so they tell you, the exceptions. "Some of my best friends are Jews."

In 1940, two years after the Un-American Activities Committee had come into existence as a Special Committee, it had become apparent that the committee did not choose to commit itself to steady, searching work. It chose, instead, to race for headlines, reckless in its accusations, careless in the definition of its duties, confused and inconsistent in its procedures. Some witnesses were permitted to read statements; others were arbitrarily refused. Some were permitted to have counsel present; others not. At some hearings, the Committee called itself a "court." At other meetings, counsel of witnesses was refused opportunity to ask questions because the members held it was not a "court."

As a special committee it necessarily had to be voted into existence with each new Congress. But at the beginning of the Seventy-ninth Congress Mr. Rankin, by a clever parliamentary move (by motion to amend the rules of the House) on the first day of the session, succeeded in establishing the Un-American Activities Committee as a Standing Committee. This meant that the committee would automatically be organized in each Congress, with no debate on its merits and accomplishments, or the need, if any, of such a committee. The Un-American Activities Committee was here to stay.

Among my papers I found the following manuscript:

From Columbia Broadcast-
  ing System
Earle Building
Washington 4, D. C.

EXCLUSIVE ON CBS
FOR RELEASE AFTER 10:45 PM, EWT
TUESDAY, JANUARY 23, 1945

REPRESENTATIVE EMANUEL CELLER SPEAKS OVER CBS ON "HOW AMERICAN WILL THE UN-AMERICAN ACTIVITIES COMMITTEE BE?"

(Following is the text of an address, titled "How American Will The Un-American Activities Committee Be?" to be made over the Columbia Network, from the studios of WTOP in Washington, by Representative Emanuel Celler, Democrat of New York, on Tuesday, January 23, 1945 from 10:30 to 10:45 PM, EWT. His talk is in the nature of a reply to Representative John E. Rankin, Democrat of Mississippi, who discussed "Why We Need A Permanent Committee to Watch Un-American Affairs" over CBS on January 16.)

184

Last week, over this station Representative Rankin looked upon his work in resurrecting the Committee o Investigate Un-American Activities—and found it good. I cannot match his enthusiasm for the past accomplishment of the Dies Committee. It did not, as far as I can see, trail any clouds of glory.

The Committee to Investigate Un-American Activities is now a standing investigatory committee with power to initiate legislation.

I mean this to be a direct talk. The vaudevillian antics, the brass band tactics, the star chamber proceedings of the Dies Committee have put all of us on notice. Bluntly then, the present committee can make its choice. It can either adopt the Dies course of unfounded character assassinations, lynch-law, prosecutor-jury and executioner all in one—or it can proceed in a manner consonant with the American tradition of the right to be heard, the right of counsel and the right of confrontation of witnesses, placing emphasis on investigation of *all* foreign isms with honest judicious objectivity. If we are to have again an extravaganza of persecution—a deep-seated mania of embracing some individually conceived notion of alienism, we face again a betrayal of our basic constitutionally guarded rights. The power to investigate is a great public trust. And we ask the newly constituted committee not for one instant to forget that.

In the final count, it remains with the American

people whether it will countenance the continuation of the former practices of the Dies Committee. Illegality will never solve the problem of political lawlessness. As we have seen so clearly demonstrated in Europe, hate breeds hate and the vicious circle revolves with all its attending madness.

Let the over-zealous be reminded of Hawthorne's description of those "who go all wrong by too strenuous a resolution to go right."

You will remember without difficulty the publicity pursuits of the Dies Committee; how reports by the chairman and paid employees, without knowledge of the whole committee, gained credence as a studied committee report; how the "Consumers' Research" was written off as a communist-front organization without a single hearing and without a single accused person called to the stand. You will recall how thousands of federal employees were publicly listed as engaged in subversive activities without even a chance to defend themselves.

Accusations get headlines; denials come too late.

You will remember the untidy proceedings of the Dies Committee concerning Goodwin B. Watson, William E. Dodd and Robert Morse Lovett wherein the committee actually succeeded in having passed a bill of attainder, that is, the imposition of punishment without a trial, an act expressly forbidden by the Constitu-

186

tion. You recall as well, I am sure, the unsavory incident of Shirley Temple, the then child actress.

From a study made of the Dies Committee and signed by over one hundred distinguished attorneys, I quote the following: "That the Dies Committee, while giving lip service to impartiality and fair play and proclaiming its devotion to Americanism and American institutions, used its hearings, the forum provided by Congress, for the dissemination of irresponsible slanders against honest public servants and private individuals and against public-spirited organizations, on testimony consisting of surmise, conjecture, unfounded opinion, unsupported conclusions and unwarranted deductions, without any attempt at verification or confirmation, which no self-respecting, fact-finding agency anywhere would consider—a proceeding wholly unworthy of the committee of the legislative body of a great and free Republic."

In a particularly careful study of the Dies Committee by Brother August Raymond Ogden published by the Catholic University of America Press in 1943 we find "The study of the Special House Committee for the Investigation of Un-American Activities indicates that the said committee is neither an ideal nor a desired means of exposing subversive activities."

Thus $625,000 dollars of the taxpayer's money has been spent mainly for looking for ghosts under the bed, to chasing only those tidbits that make lurid headline reading, to, indeed, establishing precedents in Congressional investigations that must necessarily destroy that which the committee professed to protect —namely, the democratic processes in the United States.

It has been charged that 600,000 individuals engaged in subversive activities are abroad in this land. If this is actually so, then the Dies Committee has been woefully derelict in its duty. How many convictions have been obtained because of the work of the Dies Committee? How many of those alleged 600,000 are now lodged in jail? I fear me that the Dies Committee has labored like the mountain and has not even brought forth the mouse.

I want to point to another instance which has just come to light. A political advertisement inserted in the San Francisco *Chronicle* of Monday, October 30, 1944, carried an accusation of Communism against Representative Frank Havenner running for Congress in which was set forth unsupported testimony given before a so-called Dies subcommittee on July 16, 1940 in Beaumont, Texas, at which Mr. Dies was the only member of the committee present. On January 11, 1945, Mr. Havenner, Representative from California, rose on the floor of the House and stated, among other things: "At the time of this meeting I was a Member of the House of Representatives and had been for three and one-half years next proceeding that date.

188

I had never received any notice of this hearing prior to the time it was held and have never received any notice of the hearing from the Special Committee on Un-American Activities or from any other person up to the present time. The first knowledge I had that such a subcommittee meeting was held was more than four years later when I read this political advertisement. . . . I have never been given an opportunity to appear before that committee to face my accuser or to reply to his testimony. If the chairman of the committee believed that this sworn testimony was true it was his duty to report it to the House of Representatives and recommend that I be brought before the bar of the House and expelled. If there was any doubt in his mind as to the truth of this testimony, it certainly was his duty to notify me and call me before his committee to disprove the testimony, if I could . . . instead the record of this secret meeting was pigeonholed for more than four years, when suddenly and mysteriously it was made available for use against me in political campaign."

The whole episode speaks for itself. I might add here that only through a newspaper article published the other day did I find out that I, together with Senator Pepper of Florida and Senator Thomas of Utah and other members of the House, am the subject of one of the Dies Committee's files.

Let the committee be guided by a true knowledge

and understanding of the individual rights of citizens. Because a man does not agree with you is no basis for calling him un-American. It was for this very purpose, this protection against governmental tyranny, the Bill of Rights, was written into the Constitution.

Secret investigations against private individuals, organizations, individuals in government and members of Congress without opportunity of rebuttal are Gestapo methods. We want none of that here. Consider its danger to parliamentary government in the United States when members of Congress investigate other members of Congress, making accusation against them without their knowledge and without opportunity of defense and discussion. It is a tragic threat against the freedom of expression and the free exchange of thought both in and out of the halls of Congress. It is a stifling of freedom of speech and press. The fear of reprisal, secretly activated, may deter many an honest expression of thought. The consequences to democratic processes can be foreseen by every thoughtful American. Congress would become a House divided subjected to civil strife.

There is no static definition of Americanism. There must be fluidity in political thought as well. Otherwise, we become robots and automatons. But Dies' theory was to smite and destroy all who disagreed with him.

I very sincerely desire to see the new committee do

a good job and I just as earnestly want the American people to watch how and why that job is being done. Ultimately, it is your duty, a personal charge, to guard against the abuse of power which you the people of the United States delegated to Congress.

I do not want to speak in premature condemnation. There is work, much work to be done in uncovering subversive activities in the United States. The scope of a Congressional investigating committee is wider and freer than the scope, let us say, of the FBI or a court of law which are rigidly bound by the strict rules of evidence. The standing committee can work harmoniously with the executive branches of the Government. It is no secret that the Department of Justice could not work with the Dies Committee which so often tumbled all over itself to spill some juicy item for headline purpose before full evidence was gathered. The Attorney General called the Dies Committee a "committee of espionage."

The new committee can and must work as a whole committee without permitting the self-aggrandizement of one member or two above all others. The bias and bigotry and special peeves of individual members cannot take precedence over the considered judgment of the whole committee. At the very least, unlike the Dies Committee, when one member of the committee speaks to the public or to the press, he should do so with the knowledge and consent of all the committee.

191

It is the judicious mind that the committee needs most. Its counsel and investigators should be chosen only after the most careful scrutiny as to their impartiality and their ability to separate the wheat from the chaff. Irresponsible informants, indeed all informants, should be made to submit their complaints in writing and under oath lest the committee be turned into a nice comfortable back room where each personal little axe can be ground. Hearsay and unreliable testimony must be given its proper weight and the right to cross-examination should not be denied.

The new committee should not cry out against one ism to the exclusion of others. It must not focus its attention only upon Communists and overlook the Fascist and Nazi dangers—and vice versa. We have as much to fear from one ism as from the other.

The new committee dare not withhold its fire against the many anti-Catholic, anti-Semitic, anti-union, anti-Negro propaganda groups and especially those bigots who peddle the anti-religious and anti-racial poison under the false label of "constitutional" and "good" government.

If the new committee remembers that it is a committee and not a backdrop for a one man show, much useful work can yet be done.

It is fervently to be hoped that the Dies Committee will have served at least one useful purpose in its sorry career, that of being a constant reminder to the committee how *not* to conduct its affairs.

That such words should have had to be spoken is a blot upon our history. That we face the necessity of saying over and over again, "Beware; our civil liberties are in danger," is a national tragedy.

In 1945 I thought it was possible to ridicule the climate created by the techniques of the Un-American Activities Committee. In a press release of January 9, 1945 I asked:

> Is it un-American to get up on the *left* side of the bed in the morning? If so, should all bedrooms in America be rearranged to avoid this subversive tendency?
>
> Is it un-American for Santa Claus to wear a *red* suit? Does he just wear those white whiskers to fool the kiddies?
>
> Is it un-American to be caught walking on the left side of the thoroughfare? If so, is any excuse valid? Should miscreants be thrown in the cooler?
>
> And Little Red Riding Hood, what was she thinking of, tearing around in that outfit? Were there really eggs in that basket or was it the Communist Manifesto cut up into a jigsaw puzzle? Was it really a wolf or Joe Stalin in a new snow suit?
>
> It all adds up to one thing. We must eliminate

the source of all these vexatious problems—*The Little Red School House must go!*

But the ball was rolling too fast for ridicule.

For over a decade I've watched this climate of fear grow, fathered in the beginning by this committee. Its tactics and procedures were copied in several State legislatures. The Executive, in answer to the accusations of some members of Congress, fashioned a loyalty program, whereby the accused could not know what he was accused of, did not know who accused him, could not confront his accuser or cross-examine. Legislation was passed by Congress permitting summary discharge from Federal employment in the interests of internal security, without opportunity to know or answer the charges. Employees were labeled "disloyal" or "security risk." Nobody yet has succeeded in finding the definition of "un-American," "subversive," "security risk." Nobody should be compelled to prove a negative. There were universities which began to demand loyalty oaths of their teachers.

Dozens upon dozens of bills were introduced in the Congress—bills to:

Authorize the payment of awards to informers giving information leading to the arrest and conviction of certain Communists;

Provide for the detention and prosecution of Communists and former Communists, to provide

194

that peacetime espionage may be punished by death;

Fix permanent bail of $1,000,000 for each day a convicted Communist remains away from jail;

Require the Attorney General to compile and maintain a list of subversive organizations;

Prohibit justices and judges of the United States from testifying as to the character or reputation of any person;

Deny bail on appeals from convictions in capital cases;

Amend title 28, United States Code, to require Federal grand and petit jurors to take an oath of allegiance.

The bills I have named specifically were given to the Judiciary Committee to consider.

There was a total contradiction in this picture. Liberty was beginning to be defined as giving more and more power to the state to oppress and suppress the individual; not the liberty which was born in the battle against the tyranny of the state, so that individuals could talk freely, write freely, pray freely, and assemble freely. These bills were aimed against the Bill of Rights, aimed to make the individual powerless before the machinery of the state's prosecution. Some of these bills made it a crime to talk in such a way as to "weaken the United States Government." Just what that phrase meant, like the words "un-American" and "subversive," could not be defined in or out of a court of law.

I remember how many times we talked "government" when I was a child. Friday nights as I have told were open nights at the Celler household. These were nights of music and talk. Each of the children played an instrument, and we all performed bravely for our visitors. But when the violin was put away and the piano closed, the elders talked. It was talk of anarchy, of socialism, oligarchy, atheism, capitalism. All the talk revolved around the subject of which form of government could serve the individual best. They reformed the world every Friday night and came back again the following week to tear it apart once more. Nobody feared that discussion would or could corrupt. It was healthy and it was honest. I took it for granted, as we all seemed to then, over the coffee and fruit my mother brought to the table, that discussion was a good thing. As my father said almost invariably after the visitors left, still talking, "Let them blow off steam; it will do us all good."

I remember Union Square and Columbus Circle and Bryant Park and how I absorbed the soapbox oratory with panaceas for all ills, ranging from vegetarianism to physical culture, to Christian Science, to socialism, to the eight-hour day, to workmen's compensation, and so on, and so on, and so on.

196

Since the end of World War II I have sat in my seat on the floor of the House and listened to members defend freedom of speech with an introduction of apology. It has now become almost mandatory that, as a member rises to talk on freedom of speech or assembly, he must begin it by professing his own innocence. If he wishes to speak against a bill which provides for the building of a concentration camp in the United States for subversives, he must begin, "I hate communism." The bill is not debated on its merits but is attempted to be sold to the legislators on the premise that it is an anti-Communist bill. If you are against the bill, you say it will aid Communists; if you are for the bill, you say it will hurt Communists. If a rumor is circulated that so-and-so is a Communist, the question forms itself, not "How do we know he is?" but "How do we know he is not?"

And the fear is contagious. The State Department no longer moves freely in the negotiation of foreign affairs but is trapped by Congressional denunciation.

It is a fearful thing to behold. The style set by the Committee on Un-American Activities has spread to other Congressional investigating committees. For over a decade I have opposed the Un-American Activities Committee. I have voted against appropriations for it. What I had feared most had come to pass. In the carelessness of its work, in the senseless dust screens it had raised, in its scramble for headlines, in its fathering and nurturing of this atmosphere of suspicion, it had overlooked the serious trail which led to the door of the Alger Hisses. The grand jury in New York had already worked for ten months when the Un-American Activities Committee went into the Hiss case. By its hectic prancing, the committee had placed itself in a position where it could no longer be taken seriously by thoughtful people. Like the boy in the fable, it had called "wolf" too many times.

When the Un-American Activities Committee brought the Hiss case to prominence, it brayed loudly, "Look at how right we have been!" Now, others using the weapons of character assassination introduced by the committee grow bolder and bolder. There is always Hiss they can point to. The suspicions grow thicker and nastier. "You presume, do you not," I ask my constituents and my colleagues over and over again, "that a man is innocent until proven guilty?" And I am told, "But look at Hiss." The seed of distrust has grown into a sturdy plant.

Much has been written about the Hiss case and his tragic betrayal. Liberals have been told that we refused to believe in Hiss's guilt because of our naïveté and our unwillingness to appraise realistically the nature of Communist conspiracy; that we do not understand the nature of this evil, and hence could not believe that a man like Hiss could live a lie. This I deny. To refuse to believe one guilty until he is so proven is not naïveté nor denying the existence of criminals. Determination to get at the crime and the criminal need not turn us into a nation of under-the-bed peepers, smearing senselessly our political opponents, shouting "traitor" and "Communist" at those who excite our political displeasure. Had the Committee on Un-American Activities, from its inception, worked with precision, worked with evidence, and worked with regard for the rights of an individual, the road to Hiss would have been quicker and more direct. There was serious work to be done in the area of Communist infiltration, but the drama had been turned into a farce and the country diverted from examining realistically the sinister spy threat.

Since the Eighty-first Congress, the Un-American Activities Committee has reshaped its procedures, working with greater care than in the preceding Congresses. But the mischief had already been done. It had set the pattern, and slowly the courage ebbs away to lash out against the corrosion of the Bill of Rights.

I introduced two bills: one to provide that no Senator or Representative shall be immune from civil liability for any defamatory statement inserted by him in the Congressional Record when such statement was not actually made in the chamber of the Senate or House of Representatives; the other to authorize the Committee on the Judiciary to study the conduct of hearings before committees of the House of Representatives.

Congressional immunity is necessary to permit the work of Congress to continue, but it is no reason for a member of Congress, after receiving permission, to return to his office to write whatever he pleases and insert it in the Congressional Record, thus cloaking it with immunity. The opportunity to reply immediately is lost. Sometimes the insertion goes unnoticed for days and when the reply does come, if at all, it is too late. But I could not succeed in getting any action at all on this bill.

In the practices of committee hearings, to my mind, the greatest evil is the use of television in the committee room. Television seems to make it imperative to keep audience-interest. The dry bare facts are ignored for the quick sensational charge. There are few who can resist the temptations of the camera. I have watched members of committees, as well as their counsel, submit to this temptation. I have watched members of the committees browbeat and insult witnesses who have no recourse. These are the members of Congress that have forgotten their place as servant of the people. The use of television in the committee rooms heightens, even if only momentarily, the intense sense of importance with which the members have cloaked themselves. Television has no place in committee hearings.

Because the sentiment is growing in favor of these two bills, I believe that succeeding Congresses will legislate in some way to bring about these changes.

When I first came to Congress thirty years ago, the Red Scare was just beginning to fade away. It was still fashionable to suspect the alien, to confuse the anarchist with the bolshevist, and to rate high the informer. The pendulum has swung back again.

The people of Wisconsin, in 1952, returned Joseph R. McCarthy to his seat in the Senate. But shall we not take some small comfort in the thought that he could claim no overwhelming victory, that he ran 200,000 votes behind his party ticket, that there were some 702,992 persons who voted for his opponent, Thomas Fairchild. Perhaps we can welcome this as an omen that the pendulum is moving again to a balanced center.

Will I have to make it clear, as I write these words, that I make no brief for communism? That I plead for the millions of loyal American men and women to be permitted what is theirs by right and the very nature of their country—to breathe without fear, to speak their piece freely, and to walk without peering over their left shoulder? Have I, too, touched the hem of fear?

Chapter Ten

> *Man is the only animal that laughs and weeps; for he is the only animal that is struck with the difference between what things are, and what they ought to be.*
> —William Hazlitt: *Lectures on the English Comic Writers*

Once, at a meeting of the India League of America, somebody asked me how I could so diversify my interests, bringing to each subject the same degree of intensity. He could understand it, he said, if I concentrated on one subject at a time, moving, as it were, from room to room and shutting the doors behind me. I could talk with passion about independence for India, then turn with equal concentration to civil rights or labor legislation or the removal of trade barriers in international trade or denunciation of a plan to enthrone Otto of Hapsburg. Wasn't this a spreading of one's self so thin that it marked no more than the search for vessels into which to pour a restless energy? It was a good question.

The answer is not a simple one. The question is one that can be directed to anybody elected to Congress. A thousand fragments of what the world wants, fights, hopes for, pass into his life. He is exposed to every kind of pleading through legislative proposals, through his daily mail, through leaflets, memoranda. Into his life necessarily come sometimes unsought stories of envy, ambition, greed, as well as stories of quiet heroism, devotion, and idealism. If a member of Congress looks like a grasshopper, it is to wonder how he ever alights at all.

This is not all of the answer. There is a further question. Which of these shafts aimed at him hit home? In short, where is he vulnerable? If you were to study the record of any one Congressman (including his public statements, his extension of remarks in the Congressional Record, how he votes, what causes he adopts), you would find that no matter how diversified his interests may appear to be on the surface—and his interests are always many—there is a general consistency throughout. Out of the welter of subject matters which come before him, in the final analysis, he makes a selection, and in that selection will be found one central philosophy, an identifiable approach to life itself.

The root of my interest in India is the same as the root of my interest in labor or anti-lynching legislation or immigration or monopoly power or Israel. It goes back to Brooklyn, because Brooklyn means people of all kinds, of all creeds, of all colors. It goes back to the variety of life and living in Brooklyn, to an early-awak-ened study of contrasts in how rewards and punish-ments were meted out to people; in wondering why one walked behind a pushcart while the other ate in Lundy's. It goes back not to how people lived, but to how each person lived, to the sound of the individual voice of a man selling pretzels on a stick or to the eyes of a foreign-born woman looking with pride at her child's American report card.

It is not surprising, then, that in my political read-ing I should have felt so sharply the impact of Ma-hatma Gandhi, who sought integrity for every living entity. The large words, Justice, Peace, Plenty, Free-dom—words which have as many meanings as those who speak them wish to give—meant to him the eyes and the souls and the bellies of every living human being.

It was a quiet, short bill which I introduced in Feb-ruary of 1948 to authorize a memorial for Gandhi in the United States. It was the sort of tribute that could be expected to be made toward a figure of such inter-national fame. There was polite acquiescence to its introduction by Congress generally. Although it took from February of 1948 to the end of September 1949 (going from the Eightieth to the Eighty-first Congress) to be enacted into law, this was not the result of any over-positive opposition. It was just one of those bills about which there was no rush. But what the measure represented to me was so personal that I never could and never did publicly express the compulsion I felt in sponsoring the bill.

When Nehru came to the United States in October of 1949, arrangements were made for the two of us to meet. I found, when we did meet, that his detached, reserved deportment blocked the expression of any kind of spontaneous sentiment. He knew, of course, of my interest in India and the Indian people. What I failed to convey to him, I am sure, was my emotional tie with the struggles and suffering of India, my fascination with the culture and spirit of India, and what his writings, as well as those of Gandhi, had meant to me, not so much intellectually but in emotional overtones.

On July 2, 1946, my bill, H. R. 3517, which authorized the admission into the United States of persons of the races indigenous to India and to the Philippine Islands and their eligibility for naturalization, was signed by President Truman and became Public Law 483. What the Act did was to break down the racial bar which prevented people of India from entering this country or becoming naturalized citizens.

As I look at the calmness of the words of its legislative history set forth in the Calendar of the House of Representatives, I wonder if those viewing it can understand the storm that raged over the passage of this bill:

H. R. 3517—July 3, 1945, Reported from the House Committee on Immigration and Naturalization

October 10, 1945, Passed House

June 10, 1946, Reported in Senate

June 14, 1946, Passed Senate, amended

June 18, 1946, House asks for conference

June 21, 1946, Senate agrees to a conference

June 25, 1946, Senate agrees to conference report

June 27, 1946, House agrees to conference report

July 2, 1946, Approved. Public Law 483

The debate on the floor of the House runs through twenty-six pages of impassioned outbursts in favor of and in opposition to the bill:

Mr. Allen of Louisiana. . . . When this bill came before the Committee on Immigration and Naturalization some months ago we held hearings and we took a vote on it, and we defeated it 10 to 6. . . . Then the bill was resurrected. After all the pulling and the pressure and wirepulling and everything else that could be done, the bill was finally voted out of the committee by a vote of 6 to 9. It was voted down at first by a vote of 10 to 6. After all the pressure that could be brought, it was voted out by a vote of 6 to 9. It is here before you.

Mrs. Luce. . . . What is important is that there should not be legislation discriminating on color lines on the statute books of a country which claims to believe in no discrimination against people because of the shape of their noses or the slant of their eyes or the color of their skin. Such legislation must be taken off our books, because the greatest American principle, the very greatest principle of all, or so I believe, is that every man stands equal in the eyes of God and of Uncle Sam.

Mr. Voorhis of California. . . . Whatever you or I may like to do, whatever may be the easy attitude for us to take toward this, that or the other person or group of persons, let me tell the membership of this House that in this hour we shall either attain a reasonable approximation to human brotherhood on this earth or face the imminent possibility of the virtual destruction of human civilization, if not a large part of the human race itself. . . .

Mr. Bennett of Missouri. . . . Advocates of the policy that we should let down our immigration barriers to those people who cannot be assimilated into our population are traveling with the same

crowd of no-good do-gooders and downfallen up-
lifters who think this country should be run as a
free-lunch counter for the whole world. . . .

Mr. McCormack. Mr. Chairman, it is impossible for me to see how any member can get ter-
ribly excited or emotional over this bill, a bill
which removes a legislative insult to a people and
allows at the maximum only 100 persons out of
nearly 400,000,000 to enter the United States each
year. I wonder how we would feel if some country
by law said that no American could become an immigrant to that country. Although we might not
want any American to go to that country, it still
would be an insult to the people of America if
any country passed a law of that kind. . . .

Finally, after hours of clamor, a motion was made to
recommit the bill; that is, send it back to the Committee to meet its legislative death. The motion was defeated. Eighty-three voted to send the bill back; 207
voted "no"; 141 did not vote. Without a roll call and
on "yea's" and "nay's," the bill was passed.

The Senate passed the bill in amended form without
prolonged debate.

Somewhere in my papers I found a statement I had
made at the time of my introduction of the bill. It was
just a few typewritten pages, clipped together. It bore
no title. I cannot now recall where I made the speech;
it doesn't matter. It says some of the things I wanted to

say to Nehru. It says some of the things, inhibited as they may sound in formal language, I wrote in the margin of a book of Mahatma Gandhi's speeches. I would not change a word of it today.

In my many years as legislator, one surprising discovery stands out—and I say this with thankfulness—the cynic is hardly ever right, if at all. The cynic who, as it has been said, 'knows the price of everything and the value of nothing,' has never known the exhilaration of the fight for justice. He denies the evidence of his senses, knotting the moral fibre of his humanity. He is forever for the *status quo,* whatever it may be, for as he sees it, there can be no betterment; hence, change can only be for the worse.

I am not here to deliver a little homily. I am here to assert a belief in the essential upward struggle of peoples without and within the frame of governments. In every age, in every country, the struggle has gone forward to gain a bit here, to win a skirmish there, but the important thing to remember that the gain was made and is being made in each age, each century, each day. It is what we must remember in the hours that look black, in the years of turmoil and hatred when the forces of evil seem about to engulf and drown us. It is the cynic who is the defeatist.

We know, we in the United States, that we

210

have reached no millennium, that while our achievements in justice and equality stand as monuments to that very belief in the future of man, we have by no means reached any epitome of perfection. But we never cease our self-scrutiny to find wherein we fail, wherein we are betraying the purposes of our founders. Slowly, we forge ahead to the realization that no man, no government, no people, are islands entire unto themselves, that insomuch as what happens in one corner of the earth reverberates throughout all corners, or, to change the figure, like waves that wash one shore because stones had been cast into the waters from an opposite shore.

Here we are fighting racial arrogance. 'The United Nations are fighting,' said President Roosevelt, 'to make a world in which tyranny and aggression cannot exist; a world based upon freedom, equality, and justice; a world in which all persons, regardless of race, color or creed may live in peace, honor and dignity.' And in so saying, the President of the United States was delineating our war aims. That's a mighty large program. It means the liberation of oppressed peoples as well as the removal of discriminatory measures, not so thoroughly advertised, on the statute books of our own country.

Naturally, I have reference to the fact that for no reason save that of origin, Eastern Hemisphere

211

Indians are precluded from entering the United States under immigration quotas such as are established for other peoples already embraced within the Immigration Act of 1924, and, moreover, are precluded from becoming naturalized citizens of these United States. They were thus excluded from the family of nations that *is* the United States. Is such continued exclusion the evidence that we have not as yet purged ourselves of the ugly taint of unfounded prejudice? Is it evidence that we have not been vigilant in watching our growth to a true maturity? Is not such an exclusion an echo of the totalitarian ideology that we seek to crush today? From what Olympian heights do we point our finger and say: 'You, Welshman, you may become part of us, and you, Italian, and you, Yugoslav, and you, Iraqian, but, no, not you, Indian'! If we have erred in the past in not recognizing such exclusion for what it actually is —an insufferable act of pompous racial ego—that remains no reason for such error to continue. Several remedial bills, among them my own, await legislative action. No sound reason exists for delaying the passage of such bill, setting up an immigration quota for the Indian peoples and according them the right of naturalization. It must be passed if the sincerity of our war aims is to pass the test, a test placed before us by every oppressed

212

people on this earth who looks toward these United States for justice and equality.

The Indian peoples have joined us on the battlefield. Two million are fighting in the Army, Navy and Merchant Marine of Great Britain. They are among the dead, wounded and missing. They are producing for war, farming for war, building for the war which is ours and theirs. Can we not underscore that brotherhood away from the war-torn fronts?

The inclusion of the Eastern Hemisphere Indian in our family circle is one step forward in the progression of the world towards equality. As we view the upheaval in almost every region of the world, our consciousness gives pause before the thought of four hundred million inhabitants of the land of India who find themselves subjected to foreign rule. The pulse of the people stirs. A national consciousness arises, an awareness that whatever destiny awaits India, it must be of her own making.

Yes, there are poverty and disease in India. Agriculture and industry have not reached the highest point of development. There are divisions of class and caste. I point these out because these are the very arguments that are advanced for keeping India a subject nation. This is how India has fared, ruled from above and from *outside*. An absentee landlord sends its overseers—who must somehow manage to keep their jobs—to attend to the needs, not of the inhabitants, but of the employer. Exact tribute, divide the interest, keep the level of living low, but remember to tell them that it is for their own good.

How much of the poverty and disease could be wiped out if India as a nation could be permitted to work for itself, to pay taxes for institutions of its own, could trade freely and be traded with by all the nations of the world? No unbridgeable chasm exists in India to keep the people divided and render them unfit for self-government. There are more minorities, more unrelated languages spoken in the United States, more variance in custom and belief in the United States than there is in India, and yet out of the amalgam we have forged a mighty nation.

India has an embedded culture of its own. It has no need for the kind of 'civilization' the conqueror gave it. The nineteenth century self-pitying cry, in justification of conquest, of 'white man's burden' has often impelled me to ask in viewing India, 'Who is *really* carrying the burden?'

India is precisely what I had in mind when I spoke of the hollowness of the cynic. As the world progresses in accelerated pace as it does today towards international collaboration, towards a firmer understanding of the actual physical and spiritual nearness of one people to another, there needs be much rejoicing in the heart of India. For India, today, remains an indictment of greed and lust for power and the political bid for 'prestige.' It cannot remain so for long; indeed, we the free peoples of the world dare not let it so remain. India must march with the free nations of the world, lest we slip again into the sham pose of the cynic which breeds defeat even before it has encountered the enemy.

This, then, is the working day of a Congressman— winning one battle and losing two. On the losing side can be placed the battles for civil rights legislation. You go through the motions every session. You introduce the bills—the anti-lynching bills, the Fair Employment Practices Commission bills, the anti-poll tax bills, the statehood for Alaska and Hawaii bills. The hearings are held, the reports made. The machinery of Congress grinds up to a point—and stops. You begin again the next session; the machinery is set in motion —and stops. If some legislation gets through the House, it is stopped in the Senate. If it gets through the Senate, it is stopped in the House.

The late Sam Hobbs, a member of my Committee, used to start the proceedings of each meeting by saying, "Mr. Chairman, I move to abolish the Senate." I am sure there are two or three members of the Senate who feel that way about the House. With civil rights legislation, it has always been one House or the other which blocked passage. At times it seems never the twain shall meet.

What are we concerned with here? A man, a woman, a child. Nothing else. The house they live in, the schooling they get, the jobs they can get, the freedom from fear. There is nothing intricate about civil rights legislation, nothing subtle. It simply says you shall not exclude a man from such benefits as he could honestly obtain save for his color, his race or his creed. Yet, there is nothing simple about the passion and the fury which rage around such legislation. There are members in the House whom, I believe, no force on earth can move to favor such legislation. I do not understand it.

Nor do I understand the enmity that exists against labor in the halls of Congress. Again, it seems to me it is a matter of seeing the image of the human face in the mass word "labor." It seems to me ironic that in 1952 it should have been necessary for me to speak defiantly in defense of the laboring man and woman. At the time of that speech (recorded in the Congressional Record) I had no realization that I had struck a defiant note. It was only in re-reading it that I caught the measure of my own dismay, the measure of my defiance and, perhaps, defensiveness. I said:

"Mr. Speaker: Certainly, I am pro-labor. Labor is not a commodity. When you speak of labor as a class, you are not speaking of inanimate objects

216

like telephones or filing cabinets, shoes, or waxed paper. You are speaking of people. You are talking of people who work for a living. You are talking of people who pay rent, pay for the food their families eat, pay for their clothes, pay doctors' bills, dentists' bills, hospital bills. You are talking of people who are sending their children to school or college; who, on a salary, must maintain and protect a family group, each one keeping his family in such comfort as he can, preparing for his children a life better than the one he knew.

"When I hear somebody on the floor of the House speak out against labor, spouting about the power of labor, the excessive demands of labor, I know he has never known or has forgotten the bitterness of the struggle to make ends meet. He has never known what it means to have a sudden illness wipe out the savings of a family. He has never known or has forgotten what it feels like to see other children better dressed, better fed, than his own. He sees only a composite, blurred picture of a mass, leaving out the heart and soul of a man laboring for himself and his family.

"I have listened to the speech of a high executive in the steel industry, talking against the increase in salaries for the steel workers. The average wage of a steel worker is $75 a week. The salary of this executive so speaking was $105,000 a year. True, this $105,000 a year is before taxes, but so is the $75 a week before taxes. I make no mention of this steel executive's other income from investments and rents; I do not know about them. But I do know that the laborer, earning an average of $75 a week, has no capital so that he can make his money work for him. When the executive of Inland Steel, Mr. Randolph, in his speech, asked the question, 'Is your boy making $1.70 an hour in Korea?', thereby impugning the patriotism of the steel worker and making a comparison where absolutely no comparison exists, my impulse was to rise and ask him, 'Are you?'

"The average wage in all industry, including overtime payment, is $1.65 an hour. If we deduct 5 cents from this figure (the five cents representing overtime), we then find that on a forty-hour-a-week basis, the average wage is $64. It has been estimated that it costs a family of four for the absolute necessities of rent, food, and clothing an average of about $50 a week to live, leaving $14 each week for savings, taxes, illnesses, entertainment, a luxury item here and there. In the durable goods field, the average wage is $68 a week. Each increase in price presents a problem to the average worker. It becomes not a question of what to buy but a question of what not to buy, when butter, milk, eggs, and bread keep rising in price.

"The propaganda mills pour out reams of words

about the power of labor—that the demands of labor will ruin the country; that labor is a bad, bad boy who has only his selfish interests at heart; that organized labor is Public Enemy No. 1. We hear far less about the power of management and the growth of the concentration of industry in the hands of a few. Many industries are dominated by three or four companies, which control the market and control in turn the prices the public must pay for their commodities. I hear very little said, if anything, about the common cause which management, throughout all industry, serves—to keep wages down and profits up. This is understandable. But when labor organizes in a common cause, seeking benefits by way of increased wages and better working conditions, this is called 'the crippling power of labor.'

"It was not so long ago—and the memory is still fresh with us—that practices of management—'yellow dog' contracts, the lockout, a ten-hour day, the ex parte injunction—crowded labor into a corner, depriving them of their every weapon in their advance toward a living wage.

"Even today, with the more humane court decisions and legislation, the proportion of profits for management far outruns the proportion of wage increases. Compare the strength of management with labor. Management has its huge capital, its plants, its powerful advertising outlets, its integration with other industry. Each laborer has only his two hands and his union. The battle cry is often raised to the effect that we are dealing with big unions and that industry-wide bargaining is an evil. Industry-wide bargaining is a logical development from the growth of big business in this country. Of what effectiveness would a strike be against a single plant of a huge entity when the other plants of the company can continue working, although the single plant is not operating? You might just as well say flatly that labor has no right to strike at all.

"When the National Labor Relations Act was passed during Roosevelt's administration, it was sought thereby to bring the rights of labor closer into balance with the rights and the powers so ruthlessly exercised by management. It is ridiculous to say, as is now being said, that the pendulum has swung in the other direction, and that labor is more powerful than management. The laborer has advanced step by step, paying price upon price for the small gains he has made. Each gain has taken years to secure. Can we in all honesty now say—when the average industrial wage is $64 a week in an era of inflation—that the worker is all powerful and secure? When the average worker at the age of sixty-five finds himself excluded from the labor market, a dependent upon the bounty of the state or the generosity of his

220

children—do we dare to say that the laborer is so secure and so powerful that he needs no friends? Can we now say that the laboring man is so secure and so powerful that we must now write legislation to curb that power—legislation like the Taft-Hartley Act, the sole purpose of which is to restrict the laboring man's right to strike? I am for the repeal of that act. How many laboring men can face the prospect of old age, secure in the knowledge that his savings have been sufficient to take care of his wants when he no longer can work? Is he so safe and so overpowering that when mine safety legislation is introduced in the Congress it is again and again voted down to protect the interests of the mine owners rather than the lives of the miners? Is labor so powerful that it can request and receive of the Congress of the United States a decent price-control law under which he can live? And is he so powerful and secure that he can request and receive from Congress decent housing at a rental which he can pay? On the contrary, labor has too few followers in Congress.

"You can search the records of this Congress and you will find out how little there is of legislation which passed that pointed to concern for the welfare of the working man. Taxing, housing, control legislation easily reveal how few friends labor really has."

I look back at the curve of time. Thirty years ago, when I first came to Congress, the implacable hostility of the Congress to labor interests was as evident as it was uncombatable. Between the years 1922, as I recall, and 1932, only one major act was passed in the interest of labor. This was the Railway Labor Act of 1926, which required employers to bargain collectively and not discriminate against the employees for joining a union. It also provided for the settlement of railway labor disputes through mediation and voluntary arbitration and fact-finding boards.

In 1932 the Norris-LaGuardia Act became law, which, in the main, prohibited Federal injunctions in labor disputes, except as specified, and outlawed the "yellow dog" contracts. I remember vividly the debates on the floor on this bill. I have gone back to them to catch the flavor of enthusiasm that surrounded its adoption.

I have reviewed the debate on the National Labor Relations Act of 1935 (Wagner Act), which established the first national labor policy protecting the right of workers to organize and to elect their representatives for collective bargaining. I have reviewed the debate on the Public Contracts Act (Walsh-Healey Act) in 1936, which established labor standards on government contracts, including minimum wages, overtime compensation for hours in excess of eight a day or forty a week, child and convict labor provisions, and health and safety requirements. I have reviewed the debate on the Fair Labor Standards Act of 1938, which provided minimum wages and time-and-a-half for time over forty hours a week.

It was hardly possible for me to believe that such enthusiasm had at one time existed. Labor had had its brief romance with Congress. By 1943 the age-old hostility against labor had returned.

I am setting down some passages from the debates on the Norris-LaGuardia Act and the Wagner Act to prove, if only to myself, the contrasts in climate. I have not named the speakers because the identity of each speaker is not at issue. The contrasts are:

Norris-LaGuardia Debate, March 1932

". . . Why should the employers be permitted to organize for their mutual benefits, but the laboring man be denied that privilege? The laboring man, because of his situation financially, and with dependents to support, is generally unable, single-handed, to cope with employers as to the substance of the contract between them and is compelled to agree to provisions in contracts which take from him that right which is so necessary to place him on a basis where he may exact fair and reasonable treatment for himself. Why should the employer be given legal sanction to demand by contract those things which do not in any way affect the ability of the laborer to perform his work, but which seek to shackle and en-

223

slave him in his right to demand fair and honest terms of employment? Under present conditions, when the employer deals with individuals, he may exact terms which are unreasonable and unfair to the employee; but if the employer must meet the laborers in collective strength, generally, he is required to contract fairly and with due regard for the rights of laborers to earn their living by honest toil."

". . . Congress should write into the law of the land that unjust discriminations against labor by capital shall not continue to exist; that contracts depriving the individual of the right to properly protect his own interests with fair and honest dealings shall not continue to receive legal sanction; that capital shall not crush labor with a despotic hand under the protecting arm of the law; but labor shall be placed on an equality with capital by permission to organize for mutual protection, the great weapon available to labor to secure fair and honest dealings, and when the laborer is thus clothed he may stand on an equality with his employer before the law." [Applause.]

". . . I want to felicitate organized labor and to congratulate the country upon this legislation soon to be enacted by this Congress. Our organized fighting army for economic freedom is organized labor. That army is fighting for the free-

224

dom of the great unorganized masses of the people.

"Something has been said here that the public has an interest in this legislation; in the control, through court injunction, of the conduct of organized labor. I agree with that statement, but I want to say that that public interest is in seeing that the shackles are stricken from the hands of labor, in order that the great masses of the people may enjoy the benefits that will come to them as a result of the fight that labor is making for its own release from wage slavery.

"It has been the policy of the employers of labor at all times to seek to prevent the organization of those who labor for wages in order that they might deal with that class of people as individuals and to destroy the collective bargaining power of the workers. It is the same policy that has been pursued as to the agricultural producers of the country. We find hostility toward the agricultural marketing act, which seeks to place in the hands of the farmers the collective bargaining power just as organized labor through its power has assumed that privilege." [Applause.]

". . . I do not know how many Members of this House are familiar with the operations of the so-called 'yellow-dog' contract, nor whether any of you have ever been the victims of such contracts.

225

If you will pardon a personal reference, I will take you back a quarter of a century ago and give you my experience. I was a member of a craft that worked from daylight to dark, twelve hours each day, in the region of the Great Lakes ports along the dock unloading the mammoth lake boats carrying iron ore from Duluth to Cleveland, and other lake ports. By the power and force of organized labor we were able to bring the working day from twelve hours down to eleven hours a day; and when in an effort to better our working conditions our union urged the employer to agreement by collective bargaining to a ten-hour work day, we were met with a flat denial and the alternative proposition of signing so-called contracts, which are known to-day as the 'yellow-dog' contracts, which permit the employer to treat with the individual in each respective contract."

Wagner Debate, June 1935

". . . Those are the unfair labor practices. As my colleague, the gentleman from New York, said in his brilliant speech today, what about the national trade associations? The employers' associations—they can bargain collectively among themselves. Nobody steps in and says that they cannot organize. Nobody stepped in when they came down to write the codes of the National Industrial Recovery Act, and said to them that they

226

had no right to organize and bring all their tradesmen down, their representatives of their organizations, to fix prices and take care of their own interests, and in those codes exploit the workers. No indeed! Antitrust acts did not apply to them, the antitrust laws were only invoked to enjoin workers from striking on the grounds that they were interfering with the free flow of interstate commerce. Well, what is sauce for the goose is sauce for the gander, and it is about time that we begin to realize that labor disputes do not originate with the workers but ninety times out of one hundred begin by the employer exploiting his workers by starvation wages and long, inhuman hours of work.

"Nobody raised a finger against that, but when labor comes in and says that all we want is the right to go into a booth in a factory and, with no interference by an employer, with no interference by our foreman, write down on a piece of paper whether we want a union of our own choosing, whether we want a company union, whether we want no union at all, that is a different matter. A great cry goes up that we are oppressing the employees."

". . . We are trying to give to the men and women of the United States the right to be free American citizens, to go about and say, 'I am master of my soul, I am not an industrial slave. I do not have to stand for any employer hiring a stool pigeon to work alongside of me to break up my union, and I am free to organize to get decent living wages to take care of my wife and my children.' That is what this bill is for."

". . . Mr. Chairman, as a Representative from an agricultural district, I think that when we shall have passed this bill we will have brought about an equality that has been a long time coming. Under the A.A.A. and the amendments thereto passed yesterday, the farmer has an equality in the tariff that he has never had before. Under this bill we shall give labor an equal position with the employer, a position labor has never had before. We have manufacturers' organizations, chambers of commerce, and many different types of organizations that give employers a chance to have agreements, and it is high time that we had a permanent piece of legislation giving to labor the power to bargain collectively and in the open. We hear much talk about the power it will put into the hands of the American Federation of Labor and the power it will put into the hands of agitators. It is my opinion that to give labor clearly and legally the right to organize and do it openly will bring about a situation where the suspicion and hatred that existed when union activities had to be carried on by subterfuge will no longer exist." [Applause.]

By 1943 the love feast was over. In that year the War Labor Disputes (Smith-Connally Act) was passed over the President's veto, an act which authorized plant seizure if it was necessary to avoid interference with the war effort. The central motif, "The Power of Labor," was to be played and re-played in the succeding years. In 1947 the Portal-to-Portal Act was approved to relieve employers and the Government from potential liability in portal-to-portal claims. In 1947 the Taft-Hartley Act was passed over the President's veto. I cannot help but pit these quotations against the others.

Smith-Connally Debate, June 1943

". . . Mr. Chairman, out of the hinterlands, on the high seas, the battlefronts, above the clouds, the people of America are watching us today—watching to see what we are going to do about the most burning issue in America. Mr. William L. Green has said the American Federation of Labor will endeavor to vote out of office any of us who support this Smith-Connally bill. I am wondering just how many members of his own ranks Mr. Green speaks for. Not all the men who carry his union cards believe in the hijacking and racketeering practices of the organization to which they belong."

". . . I say to you again it is time that Congress, the President, and those in authority take these racketeers of labor by the scruff of their necks, and give them the treatment which will convince the country and the union members that the United States Government is bigger than a few leaders with reptile stripes. This legislation should pass, and it will be a step to curb the unholy activities now perpetuated upon this Government."

". . . Government by law in this great Nation is challenged and is dangerously near a breakdown. Within the body politic, under governmental sanction and without Government control, we have permitted political organizations, under the name of organized labor, to grow to such proportions that they now threaten the sovereignty of the Government itself."

Taft-Hartley Debate, April 1947

". . . Thus it has become necessary that we enact this somewhat drastic legislation. It must be made drastic because that is the only kind of language that our present type of labor leaders seem to understand. It must be made drastic to protect the rank and file of the laboring people of this country against the excesses of their leaders. Because of the general recognition of this situation on the part of the public and Congress, this legislation is going to pass the House by an overwhelming majority."

". . . Congress has been generous to labor. It still wants to be; but the privileges Congress granted have been abused to the injury of the American people."

". . . It has been said that we have drawn a bill which recognizes and protects the rights of the public, but that in doing so we are destroying the rights of labor and turning back the clock of labor reform one hundred years. I think it is well for us to bear in mind who are making those charges. Are the workers of this country, the members of the unions, objecting to this bill? Or are the objections coming only from a few entrenched leaders of union labor who fear that their unrestrained power over the workers of America will be curtailed?

For eleven years out of our long history the working man found both a voice and an ear in the Congress. In the early eighteen hundreds labor had asked for a ten-hour day, restriction of child labor, free and equal education, and the abolition of home and factory sweat shops. When I was a young lad, a century later, the same demands were being made and had not yet been met. What manner of glibness is this talk of "the power of labor"?

There are those who reluctantly admit that labor in the past had suffered its abuses but now "labor has gone too far." Was there a fundamental change in 1932 and a reversion in 1943? I do not think so. The working conditions that were dealt with in the New Deal labor legislation were not new. Not the sweat shop, not the substandard wages, not the long laboring day. But the Congress had been frightened—and the Congress means the people—by the specter of unemployment and poverty stalking through the land. Starving faces were not new, but the numbers of them were. Again I say Congress is as responsive or hostile as public insistence or lethargy permits.

I have been among those who at times believed that it was a waste for a member of Congress to face re-election every two years. Before Congress has settled down to work, it is almost time to plan for re-election. The newly elected Congressman has barely had time to acquaint himself with the machinery of Congressional procedure before he must bid again for his constituency's favor. I believe now that the two-year provision is a wise one. The pattern of a member's voting is soon established. With the two-year term, a member of Congress cannot say as he votes, "This will be forgotten." It is well that the public temper is tested every two years for the really representative branch of Congress.

I say that if sufficient numbers of people had wanted the Taft-Hartley Act repealed in the Eighty-first and Eighty-second Congresses, it would have been repealed. It saddens me to reflect that the hostility of Congress to labor is a mirror of the public's self-same hostility. We all seem to be addicted to the same kind of thinking. "Corporations" conjures up one kind of picture; "labor," another. There goes that mass word again.

Sometimes the changes in public temper are fundamental, and again this is reflected in the majority of the Congress. This I saw most clearly in the area of foreign affairs. Thirty years ago, when I first came to Congress, the League of Nations had become only a wistful wish of its most ardent supporters. In my first campaign speeches I advocated participation by the United States in the League of Nations. But, naive as I was then, I could not help noticing how little enthusiasm this advocacy inspired. My campaign promises to do all I could to repeal the Prohibition Amendment

233

were always good for cheers and applause. But from the truck on which I stood to deliver my street corner addresses, I could clearly see that, when I started to talk about the League of Nations, the eyes of those nearest me grew glazed with boredom and the standees in the rear of the small crowds walked away. If I had had to depend on my support of the League of Nations for election to Congress, I more than merely question whether I could have won that prize.

I recall that in 1924 I attended a luncheon held by the League of Nations Non-Partisan Association, and most of the New York delegation was there. We were asked to lend our support to the League. One Congressman said he would have to poll his constituents. Another said he couldn't "afford" to state definitely that he was in favor of the League since most of his district opposed it.

It was difficult in that atmosphere to believe that only a few short years back the great debate on the League of Nations had been carried on with a violence that echoed across the country. But, as must be suspected by this time, I am stubborn. In 1924 I introduced a resolution calling for the United States payment of its share of expenses at any regular League conference in which we participated. Nothing came of that.

In 1927 I went to Paris as an official delegate to the Interparliamentary Union Conference. This is a periodic conclave of members of Parliaments of many countries. If any one experience convinced me that supranational law could succeed, this experience did. True, I was young, impressionable, eager to please and be pleased. But I caught a glimmer of the concept of one world. It was this experience which led me within the next two years to introduce a bill calling for the establishment of a Peace College to train young Americans for diplomatic posts. It is with nostalgia, with the small, empty feeling of reliving a lost dream, that I reread the idealistic statement which I issued when I introduced the bill:

The United States Peace College

We have for generations rationalized war until the habit of thought of our body politic is that wars are necessary evils which the world must endure. It will take years of real education to thoroughly supplant this 'war' idea with the idea and ideal of peace, which is the heart hunger of a vast and ever-increasing body of American citizenry. This education must be according to the most approved pedagogical methods, by teachers who are authorities, pursuing a most carefully wrought curriculum. Haphazard enlightenment, no matter how highly idealistic or splendid its motive, retards what it intends to advance.

The Kellogg treaties have fired the imagination of all right-minded citizens. The famous pact does not prevent wars, but makes them illegal. It is probably the greatest step in furthering the cause of world peace ever advanced. It fixes the international mind upon the possibilities of peace because of the power and authority of the originator and its signatory acceptances in Paris.

But epoch-making as it is, it never will come to full fruition until backed by a strong national public opinion. We must mold a strong public opinion favorable to it. This in turn requires the education of public opinion.

Agreed that education is the most efficacious method, where shall we start? Shall we leave the matter in the hands of well-intentioned enthusiasts?

Inimical to the best results in molding public opinion is the fact that individuals speaking as such are accepted as individuals and their teachings commonly accepted as individual opinion but lacking in authority. Let us honor the good they do and be grateful to those who finance them, but not be blind to their limitations.

If it is worth while to set up institutions and man them with the best available brains for the training of young men in the arts and the practice of war, how much better is it to set up as comprehensive, as well-manned and adequately organized institutions in the arts and practice of peace. If it is worth while to organize our citizenry into a great unit for the prosecution of war to its earliest success, how much more worth while is it to organize and train them for ultimate permanent peace.

Would it not be an epoch-making step, if our Government, safeguarding the best interests of all of its people, continued its War College and its Naval Academy with their present high standards, but matched them with a Peace College.

A Peace College attracting young men who would be taught all of the arts of peace, including diplomacy; men who could be guaranteed in the cause of peace as high a place as those now trained for war; men who could be given preference in diplomatic appointments; such an institution would be the crown of the American Educational System.

Men trained in the arts of peace would be continuously drafted for the education of the public in various ways. Speaking as they would with authority after such training, through the radio and other channels, they would become a tremendous factor in molding public opinion in favor of universal peace.

A Peace College should be distinctly the work of the Government. A few millions thus spent would mean a saving of billions, if one war was prevented, to say nothing of the preservation of countless thousands of precious lives, homes and property.

To this end I have introduced a bill to appropriate one hundred thousand dollars to be expended by a committee of five to be appointed by the President to find ways and means whereby such an institution can be established.

Gradually, at first almost imperceptibly, public temper started to change. A note of urgency crept into the mail and into the scattered one-minute speches on the floor. The Fascist and Nazi rise to power brought into discussion a vital question. To what degree does the internal policy of a foreign government concern the United States? The asking of that question was the first turning toward internationalism. But it could be seen that the turning was slight, so slight that when President Roosevelt made his "quarantine speech" in Chicago in 1937, it met with little response. As late as 1940 the Presidential candidates, Wendell Willkie and Roosevelt, made no commitment toward intervention. This was so, notwithstanding President Roosevelt's granting of fifty destroyers to Great Britain in exchange for bases in September of 1940.

Shortly after the 1940 election, it became clear that the country was split between the isolationists and the interventionists. By that time the wheel had turned half-way, but no more.

I was not to see the wheel making the turn. The last month of the year 1940 and eight months of the year 1941 were to find me hospitalized with the illness the doctors called epidural abscess, leading to osteomyelitis of the vertebra. It all began with a barber plucking an ingrown hair on the cheek. One week after that I was brought to the hospital and there, after a succession of operations, I remained for five months. I was returned home and within ten days was brought back to the hospital.

I remember nothing of those days except the almost unendurable pain that enveloped me each time I regained consciousness. Most of those months I was sunk in a coma. It had been the almost unanimous verdict of all the physicians, I was told later, that recovery was impossible. Finally, after about six months, Dr. William Linder of Brooklyn, one of the country's ablest surgeons and now gone to his eternal reward, was called in. He decided to operate once more. After this fifth operation recovery set in. This infection of a disc in the spine came before the days of penicillin, a drug which would have removed forthwith the disease and the pain. Instead scraping and cutting were essential.

As I slowly gained strength Stella and the nurses told me how difficult I had been. In my delirium I had expected every nurse to be a foreign correspondent. I kept asking questions about the Congress, about Germany, about Great Britain. Once I insisted that the nurse on duty at three A.M. call Steve Early at the White House. Another time I had said to the nurse, "Take this letter down." It was a long, rambling, incoherent, effusive outpour to President Roosevelt. When I finished I said, "Now read it back." The nurse fled in fear. I was told that the nurses whispered among themselves about this tyrant of a congressman. One of the nurses asked Stella, "How can I know whether President Roosevelt is going to change the Secretary of State?"

When I was finally permitted to leave the hospital, there began a time of reading and thinking to catch up with the events which had marched beyond me. There was scarcely time. The debate on intervention was raging at a pace I had not encountered before.

The rest is history. By the end of World War II the revolution of the wheel toward collective security was almost complete.

It cannot be said that the acceptance of internationalism was the result of an orderly thought process from premise to conclusion. Understandable contradictions ran through the voting record of a good many members. My own voting record reveals inconsistencies which prove "A man's a man for a' that." If my unyielding support for the United Nations Organization is a matter of fact, so is it a matter of fact that I voted against any increase in the size of our armed forces in 1948. And while I favored the Marshall Plan in 1948 and later Mutual Security Administration assistance and N.A.T.O., I declared myself opposed to military and economic aid to China and Spain, as well as to the Truman doctrine giving aid to Greece and Turkey. There were reasons I held for such action, which I have explained elsewhere—perhaps not always now to my own satisfaction. Perhaps I can say the same of my opposition to post-war aid to Britain and can explain it on the ground of my emotionally violent reaction to British foreign policy in Palestine, in India, and in Ireland.

Certainly I have watched the people of the United States and myself, as one typical of the people of the United States, slowly and painfully groping toward maturity, toward the acceptance of responsibilities the avoidance of which leads to stagnation and atrophy and, ultimately, to the self-destruction that comes through flight from reality.

The course and the growth of the country are the course and the growth of the people, not people massed together, but seen as identifiable units. The growth is painful because the grasping of responsibility does not grow out of a wish to do so or by deliberately following the plans of a carefully drawn blueprint. The growth comes out of necessity when there is no alternative. It is either to accept the responsibility or to wither. Nowhere is this more clearly seen than in the foreign policy of the United States.

President Truman's relation with Congress was not a happy one. He was opposed bitterly by the Southern members of his own Party and he was opposed equally as bitterly by the Republican Party. Yet it is of inescapable significance that the major foreign policy program was adopted by Congress and enacted into law despite debate of frenzied opposition. This was done, too, it must be noted, despite the virulent and unceasing attacks upon President Truman's Secretary of State, Dean Acheson. It will be a point upon which many future historians will ponder as they search the record. The loud, angry, raucous charges against Dean Acheson, the desperate struggle of the Republican Party, so long out of power, to make itself heard, will be matched against the success of bills fathered by President Truman and the Secretary of State, which became the foundation of our foreign policy. It hurt, but it had to be done. The necessity was upon us. The word "isolationist" had become an epithet.

In 1945 in a radio address I had said:

"I do not wish to be misunderstood. It is not my purpose to do any special pleading on behalf of Russia. I am not rushing to the defense of her political system. Most certainly I want no part of her brand of government in the United States. I want no part of communism. First and foremost, we are a democracy with the best kind of government suited to the needs of our country. Russia continues in her system which she deems best. That is not the issue here, not the issue at all. The issue is the direction so many of our opinion moulders are taking, that of regarding Russia, if not as our present enemy, then as our potential one. Instead of bending our efforts tirelessly toward the creation of world peace, a peace durable and strong, we stand in danger of losing our perspective, our balance. We curb neither our tongues nor our tempers, and our patience, put to the test, has proven entirely too thin. This is as true of Russia as it is of us."

This is what I had wanted to believe and, in part, it is what I still believe, what most of the people of the United States want to believe. Not a turning away from the recognition of the existence of evil and evil intent, but a belief that evil can be restrained legally and morally through collective strength, through patient negotiation (although it means at times being reduced to frustration and impotent rage), through treaty, and through the United Nations. All these things together not only can be, but must be, tried. Only after these have failed and only when there is no alternative—no other single honorable alternative that

243

wise and patient men can devise—can we dare to talk of the inevitability of war.

We wanted so desperately during the war and immediately afterward to return to the ways of peace. So intense was this desire that we naturally assumed the same fervent wish on the part of the Soviet Union. We had seen so much of murder and war, the crushing of men's souls, that there were many (and I count myself among those) who believed that no country wished to see them again. We were wrong—for the right reasons. There were a few who were right for the wrong reasons.

Maybe it is asking too much of us, maybe we lack the capacity, to look at an ugly fact directly and squarely until we fall over it and smash our noses.

In 1950 I addressed the Men's Club of Kew Gardens, New York. By no means could it have been considered a major address, or one on which, in the ordinary course of daily activities, I would have spent many hours of preparation. The subject was "The Future of the United Nations." I was and am "sold" on the United Nations. Into that one speech, before a small group, I put more of myself, more of what I believe, than I have into any other speech I have ever made. That is a tall statement, but I do not exaggerate. I set the speech forth now, uncut and un-edited, because no story of myself could be complete without it.

THE FUTURE OF THE UNITED NATIONS

I have no crystal ball. I have no gifts of clairvoyance. I cannot give myself the luxury and comfort of saying that this or that will happen, that given one set of conditions, others will follow inevitably. But what we do have, you and I together, is the hope and the desire for a secure and a permanent peace.

This is not a happy world. These are years of tension and anxieties. These are the years that require greater courage on our part than any other years in history, courage to face the fears and the tensions. This is the era of decision.

Because of our wealth, our resources, our power, we have assumed world leadership or, shall I say, it has been thrust upon us. The role of leadership does not mean—and this thought must be made evident in every portion of the world—that we stride across two oceans like a huge colossus tramping on the pride of peoples less fortunate than we. All of us know the type of man who gives and brags, and all of us know the resentments and the dislikes he leaves in his wake. It is up to us to realize that we are one in a family of nations, that the rights and the securities of these nations are as dear to them as our rights and securities are dear to us, that no nation, like no man, is an island unto itself. Peace and security can no more be achieved by one nation by itself than can the waters touch one shore and not the other. The ivory tower of isolation has crashed to the ground. This is what President Truman meant when he said in his report to Congress on the United States participation in the United Nations, "that support of the United Nations *is and must be* Point 1 of our foreign policy."

I am convinced that the future of the United Nations means the future of the world. I know there are many to whom the United Nations appears as merely a debating society. I know there are many to whom the seemingly endless discussions in the United Nations are frustrating and infuriating and that it appears to them to be a puny Tower of Babel adding more confusion to an already confused world. Nothing could be further from the truth. What these people fail to realize is that only the man with a whip, without respect for the integrity and differences of others, moves quickly. His is the rule by fear and a rule which must ultimately destroy itself. Yes, it is a maddening slowness to many of us, but then neither people nor nations are checkers to be pushed around a board by the masterminds.

It is amazing how quickly some will seize upon the evidence of failure and turn aside from the successes. The areas of disagreement are stressed and never the areas of agreement. Never let it be said of us that we prefer the battleground to the table of conference. That is the basic principle of the United Nations—

moving away from the battleground to the conference table. So it has done with the Indonesia dispute, with the Palestine dispute and with the Kashmir disputes. The United Nations Commissions in these areas succeeded in establishing truces which might otherwise have ended up in the battlefields growing larger and larger and larger.

For more than two years the situation in Indonesia had been of grave concern to the international community. Through the intervention of the United Nations, an agreement was reached between the Netherlands and the Republic of Indonesia for the end of hostilities, the establishment of a new and independent Indonesian nation, and the formation of a voluntary Netherlands-Indonesian union. Today the Republic of Indonesia is the sixtieth member of the United Nations.

Through the mediation efforts of the United Nations, Israel has signed four truce treaties with its warring neighbors. Israel was the first Republic of international birth. True, the United Nations is faced now with determining the status of Jerusalem, but I am confident that the United Nations will realize how unrealistic and incapable of implementation would be the internationalization of the City of Jerusalem.

In Kashmir the cease-fire order of the United Nations on January 5th led to a truce between India and Pakistan whose disagreement over the position of

Kashmir had caused the loss of thousands of lives in the fighting between the two countries. Though no definite agreement had been reached between the two countries, the fact still remains before us that the dispute has moved from the battlefield to the conference table.

These have been no small achievements of the United Nations. The course has not always been straight, consistent, and firm, but there was and there still is a working through to these problems which are like scattered lights coming through in the darkness.

The story of Korea proved conclusively the vitality that lies within the framework of the United Nations. Fifty-three nations moved together to oppose aggression and thereby gave heart to a world waiting fearfully for acts of decision.

Certainly all is not sweetness and light, neither in Indonesia nor Israel nor Kashmir nor Korea. None of these stories can yet be concluded with: "And they lived happily ever after." But to minimize these and other achievements of the United Nations is to deny the evidence that the United Nations can grow into the most potent force for peace and security above any other one factor in the world today.

Obviously there are weaknesses in the structure of the United Nations—weaknesses that have been made apparent by the insatiable appetite for disagreement possessed by Russia. Russia has used the veto power fourteen times in the Security Council. She has thus been able to paralyze the Security Council again and again by negative votes. The decisive action on Korea could never have been taken had not Russia walked out previously in protest over the non-seating of Communist China. If the United Nations is to exist as a meaningful force in the world today, this paralysis must be broken.

Under the present procedure should the territory of a country that is a member of the United Nations be invaded, the permanent delegate of the United Nations of the country attacked can apply to the Security Council for action. The Council meets and brings to a vote a motion to have United Nations members rush military aid to the attacked country. Such military aid can then be blocked by a veto.

However, a new plan has been presented by the United States, which to my mind can free the United Nations to act speedily and effectively against acts of aggression. The plan calls for each of the sixty member countries to designate parts of its own Army, Navy, and Air Force equipped and maintained within the country subject to the orders of the United Nations. Teams of observers provided by UN members are to be established. They would be available on a few hours' notice to fly to any part of the world where a conflict either exists or threatens. When a UN member is attacked, he would call for an immediate meeting of the Security Council. Should the Security Council veto action against aggression, seven of the eleven council members could call an emergency session of the United Nations Assembly to take up the specific act of aggression within twenty-four hours. If seven of the council members fail to do this, any thirty-one members of the United Nations could call an emergency session. The Assembly then meeting could by two-thirds vote ask the UN members to rush UN units of their armed forces to the aid of the attacked country.

Further, under this plan a United Nations military adviser could coordinate military action pending the appointment of a Commander-in-Chief of United Nations Forces by the Assembly. The Assembly could also order teams of observers to the scene of attack.

True, this is not the perfect plan, since there could be no intervention in the event of a civil war because under the UN charter, the United Nations has no authority to intervene in the internal affairs of a country.

It may be extremely difficult, likewise, to secure sufficient votes in the Assembly for an attack by Communist China, let us say for example, on Formosa, since the recognition of Communist China has already been declared by many of the members of the United Nations.

But under this plan one of the most important objectives will have been reached, and that is the breaking of Russia's veto power in the Security Council.

Last week the Soviet Foreign Minister Andrei Vishinsky formally presented two resolutions to the United Nations Assembly Political Committee. One recommended that until the international army is created, the five powers—France, China, Britain, the United States, and Russia—should consult on joint action for maintaining international peace and security.

The second resolution recommended that the Security Council decide on measures for the rapid creation of the international armed force provided for in the UN charter and for the effective operation of the military staff committee.

The United States is in accord with these resolutions and will, I am sure, seek to combine them with its own plan which I have outlined before.

I feel, thus, that the United Nations is steadily gaining in stature and effectiveness and that its acceptance by the peoples of the world as the most potent force for peace will go further toward insuring that peace than any single act by any single country.

But when we talk of war and lose sight of *the causes of war,* we are burying our heads in the sand and are a perfect target for even a poor marksman. It is in this area—in studying and eradicating the causes of war—that the United Nations has done and can continue to do its most effective work. The work in this area has neither the drama nor the excitement which could bring it into the headlines. This work has, therefore, been so badly under-publicized that the prestige and effectiveness of the United Nations has greatly suffered.

It is generally agreed that the economic distress of a nation is one of the causes of war. Recognizing this, the United Nations has set up the Economic and Social Council consisting of twelve commissions covering such fields as employment, transport, communication, social and human rights, status of women, statistical, fiscal, population, narcotic drugs, coal, electric power, steel, timber, agricultural problems, trade, etc. There are the Food and Agriculture Organization, the World Health Organization, the United Nations Educational, Scientific and Cultural Organization, the International Civil Aviation Organization, the International Bank for Reconstruction and Development, the International Monetary Fund, the International Refugee Organization, the International Labor Organization, the Universal Postal Union, and the International Telecommunication Union—all specialized agencies which have been brought into relationship with the United Nations under special agreements.

While the Economic and Social Council and its commissions do not have the power of legislation, it can and has made recommendations to the General Assembly and directly to governments.

The Food and Agriculture Organization has brought improved varieties of corn into Europe and the Near East and better breeds of poultry into the Orient. It has conducted schools in technical subjects such as artificial insemination to improve livestock in Europe. The United Nations sent an expert to Guatemala to help establish a school of social work. The World Health Organization has assisted Greece in stamping out malaria. The International Bank for Reconstruction and Development loaned sixteen million dollars to Chile for hydroelectric development and for the purchase of agricultural machinery. Under a training program, fifty-two fellowships were granted for advanced study in Australia, Belgium, Canada, Chile, Costa Rica, Denmark, France, the Netherlands, Sweden, the United Kingdom, and the United States. Fields of study include resources development, public administration, statistics, finance and trade, hydraulics, mineral exploration, electricity production, etc.

Through the work of the International Refugee Organization hundreds of thousands of displaced persons have been resettled throughout the world and received special instruction and training while awaiting resettlement. The Economic and Social Council has made special studies of unemployment—its causes and preventions. It has accomplished the exchange of information between countries concerning the outbreak and spread of communicable diseases. Top priority has been given by the World Health Organization to such diseases as malaria, venereal diseases, tuberculosis, environmental sanitation, maternal and child health and nutrition.

I cannot dwell in detail, as you can readily understand, on these multitudinous activities. I only want to emphasize that this work of the United Nations is unparalleled in history and is opening door after door of the road to peace and security for all mankind. Tremendous problems face us individually and as members of the United Nations, but these problems are not uniquely ours. Our problems are those of the world and hence belong to the United Nations.

Among the problems before us remain the international control of atomic energy, armaments in general, controversial political problems like Spain and China, the advancement of the people of trust territories, etc. Over all falls the struggle between the East and the West. There is before us the terror of not only another war, but *another kind* of war which could let loose the destruction the world has never seen. The battle in Asia is for 1,162,881,111 souls—the greater portion of the world's population. A slumbering giant is awakening, and the turning of the giant in this direction or that can yet determine the direction of our civilization.

In the Asiatic struggle to secure its rights as human beings, the equilibrium of power could very easily be destroyed. India, with its 337 odd millions, and China, with its 463 millions of population, are the central areas of Asia. China is Communist. India is neutral. What course shall the United Nations follow in relation to both? Shall the United States, for example, recognize China and support its membership in the United Nations in accordance with both the Russian and Indian point of view—one national unfriendly, the other friendly? Is this opposition to China interpreted by Asia as a symbol of white supremacy, or is it interpreted by Asia as an opposition against totalitarianism? Is China itself capable of any peaceful international relations, though Communist? Yugoslavia though Communist is a member of the United Nations as are Russia and Poland. Should the fact that it is Communist be sufficient to keep it out of the United Nations? Is the Chinese Communist Government truly representative of its people? Is Communist China outside of the United Nations more dangerous to the people of the world than as a member of the United Nations?

These are the questions that are posed. I frankly do not know the answers. I only know that we cannot afford to be rigid, that we must face these answers and look for the truth *no matter where that truth leads*. I only know that we cannot act independently, that we must act together through and with the United Nations, throwing our weight on the side of peace without appeasement, on the side of freedom and human rights, on the side of economic and social health.

Nor can you leave these decisions to statesmen and diplomats only. You are the people. Your government is subject to your will and will act as you dictate through the opinions you express and the votes you cast. I think it is more vital now than at any other time in your life that you keep yourself informed, that you watch the developments, that you think these problems through without haste and as free from prejudice as you can make yourself.

If the United Nations is to survive, it is because you want it to survive. Yes, you are free to express your opinion, but the one plea I make is that it be an informed opinion. The responsibility we all have today is a large one, but I believe firmly that if we all proceed with a fast conviction that *war is not inevitable* and keep remembering that through all the frustrations and resentments, we can proceed with wisdom and judgment. To believe otherwise is to throw in the sponge. Man-made problems are hard, yes, but being man-made, they are solvable.

Chapter Eleven

*If the heavens were all parchment, and
the trees of the forest all pens, and
every human being were a scribe, it
would still be impossible to record all
that I have learned from my teachers.*
—Ascribed to Jochanan Ben Zakkai

What have thirty years in Congress taught me? Two
conclusions I can state with finality: (1) There is no
political fact more important than the ballot; (2) Few
voters know it.

I have watched constituents walk into my office, half-
numbed with fright. Their first moments are occupied
with the struggle of determining just how to address
me. More often than not the constituent apologizes
for his intrusion on my "valuable" time. Sometimes he
stammers; sometimes he blushes. He fails to see what
role he, as an individual, plays in a democracy. He has
elected me to serve him. His vote, added to those of
others, has placed me behind the desk which he ap-
proaches humbly. His taxes pay my salary. He is entitled to my time and to my courtesy and to my serv-

257

ices as his Congressman. His opinions and his convictions are important to his Congressman. How important, I hazard the guess, he does not know.

I have been fortunate, most particularly fortunate, in the composition of my constituency. Brooklyn has never suffered in silence, be it in baseball or in politics. Generally, my constituents leave me in very little doubt about their sentiments. But still there has not been enough of such expression of opinion, and still there are not enough voting.

There are seven members in the House of Representatives elected from Brooklyn. Yet I will hazard another guess, that only two out of every ten people who walk into my office looking for their Congressman actually reside within my district. The other eight do not know who their Congressman is. It has been my experience, however, that at least half of that eight would not hesitate to criticize how Congress has legislated, belittling it for its mediocrity, for its failure to act, or for its rashness in acting. Try it as a parlor game some time and find out how many of your friends and neighbors know the name of their Congressman. If they do know the name, ask if they know how he has voted on bills which are important to you and to your friends and neighbors.

The constituent, in too many instances, is merely a spectator of, and not a participant in, the processes of democracy. These acts of omission on the part of the constituency, either through ignorance or lethargy or the attitude of pseudo-sophistication, are as dangerous to the extension of democracy as are the calculated plans of a selected few who conspire to overthrow our democratic machinery. The constituency determines the strength or the weaknesses of a democracy. You get only that kind of Congress which indifference or interest breeds.

I can only repeat here what I have tried to particularize in the preceding pages: No legislative act—good, bad, or indifferent, according to your views—is ever thrust on a people. There is a time of ripening leading up to receptivity. There are bills which are introduced year after year and die with each Congress. Some of these bills have been reintroduced for as much as twenty and thirty years. Some are finally enacted, and then with such rapidity within one Congress that it appears little short of miraculous to those who had advocated them for twenty years back. Examples of such legislation would be the Minimum Wage and Hour Act, Social Security, the Celler Anti-Merger Bill I discussed in Chapter VIII, the Tennessee Valley Authority, the Constitutional amendment eliminating the "lame duck" Congresses, the Constitutional amendment providing for direct election of Senators. These ideas were no less valid twenty years ago than they are now. When I was a lad, the eight-hour laboring day was as bitterly fought as is National Health Insurance today. I have seen yesterday's unorthodoxies become today's conventions. There are always, to borrow Arnold Bennett's phrase, "the passionate few" who cherish and nourish an idea, pushing it forward and facing the slow, frustrating, almost defeating inertia of the years.

In Italy I was asked, "Why does not the United States do something about returning Trieste to Italy?" In my office an angry delegation of visiting constituents will ask me, "Why doesn't Congress get a stronger price control act?" There is a clear parallel between these two seemingly disassociated questions. Behind both questions lies the image of a super-authority, cracking a whip on the bare back of a horse, forcing him in a single direction. To my Italian friends I explained patiently that the United States is only one country among others, that there are differing viewpoints of different nations to be reconciled and brought to a point of agreement, that the United States can express its sympathy, give its own opinion, negotiate in one way or another, but beyond that, it cannot substitute its own judgment for the judgment of others or erase every other viewpoint but its own. To the angry constituents I patiently explain that the United States is a vast country, a country of regions, of interests that sometimes run counter to other interests—farming, export, commercial, labor, rural, city, the West, the East, the North, and the South, with their own geographical problems, all to be brought to a point of agreement. I have learned how difficult it is to spread this picture before the constituent. I know how difficult it was for me to absorb the meaning of the tug and pull of regional interests on the floor of the House, as well as that of 435 diverse personalities which constitute the membership of the House of Representatives. Legislation seldom, if ever, is the result of precise, logical thought; essentially, it is compromise.

Perhaps one of the most perplexing problems a Congressman faces is to determine whether to serve the national interest or concur in the majority, or seeming majority, of his own district. I point to the question of Universal Military Training as an example. For years I opposed Universal Military Training. This was in accord with my own views and those of my constituents. Slowly and reluctantly, forced by the reality of the Soviet threat, I reversed my position. But the preponderance of sentiment in my district, as expressed orally and in letters sent to me, was still opposed to this radical departure from the nation's tradition. Many mothers in my district organized into groups to petition me through the mail, visit me in my home and in Washington, to prevail upon me to vote against Universal Military Training. Which dictates could I follow? Those of my conscience, of my painfully arrived-at conclusion, my interest in the national security, or the dictates of those who had elected me to office to represent them?

In this connection I am reminded of the story of an irate constituent who demanded by telegram to know forthwith whether his Congressman was for or against Universal Military Training and the Congressman wired back: "I certainly am."

Once before I had faced a similar dilemma. In the Eightieth Congress President Truman had urged the Congress to adopt legislation giving military and economic aid to Greece and to Turkey. The necessity for such legislation, it seemed to me, was apparent and has more than proved its worth in the years since enacted. But my district opposed it. I sent a questionnaire to the homes of my constituency, hoping to attain a sample thereby of my district's viewpoint. The tabulation of the poll showed that residents in my district, three to one, opposed the enactment of such legislation. Following the wishes of my constituency and setting aside my own convictions, I voted against this legislation.

In the matter of Universal Military Training I voted my own convictions and not those of my district.

This is the dilemma which each Congressman faces. I am convinced now that the Congressman represents, over and above his district, the national welfare. This is the summit—the national welfare—to which he must climb. Else why a national legislature? To do otherwise, I am now convinced, balkanizes the nation. Then

262

too the Congressman must at times attempt to lead and persuade his people that the national interest should be paramount to the local selfish viewpoint.

I keep returning to the thought of how the will of the people could move mountains if it knew its own power. Each four years the people are offered a choice of presidential nominees. The nominees have been chosen at their respective conventions. For decades upon decades the American public have talked about backroom politics, the bargains, the compromises, the commitments made, which resulted in the favoring of one candidate for nomination over another. They have sounded knowing and cynical about these abuses.

Yet, a legislative remedy exists which sufficient public support could have enacted, with opposition melting away under public insistence. I have, together with others, proposed a Constitutional amendment enabling Congress to enact a Federal statute regulating the use of the primary system in a uniform manner in the nomination of the President and the Vice-President. Through the use of uniform national primaries the majority wish of the membership of the respective political parties would prevail. It would reduce the weight placed on choosing candidates, as is so often the practice, from states carrying large electoral college votes. It would mean that earnest intra-party campaigning would begin prior to the conventions and enable keener public scrutiny of the candidates offered for choice. It would prevent bloc voting at the conventions, which derives so often from local political power. Some sixteen states have such primaries. Five primary results are binding upon the delegates; the rest are not. Some states have had such primaries and have repealed them. Perhaps now, with the advent of television offering a close-up view of the nominating conventions, the people will demand—and if they demand, they will receive—the necessary legislation for the establishment of national primaries for the nomination of Presidential and Vice-Presidential candidates.

To carry this thought one step further, the establishment of such primaries will increase the interest in state primaries in which local candidates are nominated for office within the state or for the Congress. Again, the apathy and indifference of the people within the state weaken the democratic processes. People somehow have settled on the thought that the importance lies in choosing between the candidates of the different political parties, and have not grasped the significance that the selection of candidates within the party itself is just as important. In our two-party system, as it operates in the Congress, there is no clear line of party responsibility. On certain issues Democrats and Republicans cross lines without fear of losing party favor. In appropriation bills this is very common as it is in immigration legislation and civil rights. It is not an uncommon sight to see two members of the same party taking opposing positions on a bill. The ties to the party under whose banner the Congressman runs are very loose and in some instances hardly discernible. Hence, it becomes of primary importance that the electorate know as much of the candidate for office as he knows of the principles of the party itself. Ultimately, the caliber of Congress depends upon the results in the state primaries. This fact has not as yet impressed itself upon the electorate, and absence from the state primary polls is another chink in the democratic armor.

If the electorate in so many instances is ignorant of the name of its representative in Congress, how much more widespread is that ignorance of its assemblyman or state senator. Since the state organizations control the naming of those who shall represent the party in the national election, it becomes clear that the constituent's interest must begin on local and state levels.

When I was first elected to Congress in 1922, a ten to four o'clock working day was enough to meet the demands put on the legislature. Congress did not see the need for meeting more than six months out of the year. For almost ten years this state of affairs existed. But with the depression, the rise of totalitarianism, the Second World War and its bitter aftermath, the legislator's day extended to ten, twelve, and in many instances fourteen hours a day. Congressional recesses became shorter and shorter.

The constituent felt the impact of government in his home, in his job, and in his social thinking grow deeper and deeper. As the constituent's gaze turned more and more to the national scene, it turned less and less to what was happening in his own state and community. Career-conscious young men sought out Washington, bowing to the now unhappy universal attitude that state and local politics are too petty and too shoddy for their allegiance. I have spoken to many of these young men, and I am appalled at how little they know and how much less they care about their state political activities. It is a mistake, and a bad one.

The feeling of intimacy with the national government is much greater than that which people have for their own city or state. This, too, is unfortunate. My mail is heavy with letters from constituents who inform me that the traffic light is broken on their street and would I please get it repaired? Or the policeman on the beat has been discourteous and would I have him reprimanded? Or there is no public library within walking distance from the constituent's home. Or the principal of the school is anti-Catholic, or anti-Semitic, or just "anti"; would I please have him removed? I had a letter from a mother asking me to write to her son, telling him not to marry the girl he is now seeing.

266

I had a letter from a father, asking me to introduce his son to Irving Berlin because he had a beautiful voice. These are typical of part of the mail received in every Congressman's office.

The interest in the national government, stirred to expression by the magic of Roosevelt's personality, was one of the healthiest evidences of the lusty life of a democracy. But it has now swung too far. The states shed more and more of their responsibilities as the people look more and more to the national government. Because of their indifference to state administration and state politics, the people themselves have encouraged the growth of the central government to a point where the lines between state responsibility and national responsibility stand in danger of being erased. I am not making the point that there is too much awareness of the national government. I am, however, making the point that there is too little awareness of state government.

There are deficiencies in our representative government in Congress which, while they have been noted and written upon for many years, have not been remedied because of the lack of public insistence. The Electoral College system of electing the President and Vice-President, on the one hand, gives an unfair advantage to the populous states, which the rural states do not have in the election to the two highest offices in the land. On the other hand, the apportionment of representation in the Congress given to the states at present gives an unfair advantage to the rural population. Unfortunately, these two do not cancel out the advantages one group has over the other.

Representative government demands that each constituent's vote have the same weight. At present, each state for itself determines how it shall apportion the number of Representatives it has been accorded under the national law based on the decennial census. State legislatures, therefore, have tended to mark out Congressional districts in a manner favoring the party in power. For example, one district in the State of Ohio is so outlined that the Congressman from that district represents some 900,000 constituents, while another district in that same state contains 200,000 constituents. Yet the vote of the member representing only 200,000 carries as much weight as the vote of the member representing 900,000. Also, going back to the district of 900,000, each constituent's vote electing this member is of infinitesimal weight compared to the weight of the constituent's vote in the district of 200,000. In shaping these districts, some of the state legislatures, in order to secure a preponderance of one-party domination, have resorted to flagrant gerrymandering. Some districts on the map look like the outlines of a shrunken rabbit, others like fluttering wash on a line, and others like a twisted donkey tail.

Such apportionment has resulted in many instances

in the concentration of Congress on legislation most favorably viewed by agriculturalists. This fact has been most clearly indicated by the vote on legislation concerning price and rent controls. At the same time, the Congress has reflected (in terms of relative populations) a disproportionate disapproval of legislation benefiting labor.

The Electoral College system, in contrast, demands that campaigning be concentrated in heavily populated states. In effect it disenfranchises the minority votes of all states which, when added up, could possibly change an election return. Twice the House of Representatives has elected a President contrary to the popular vote. It can easily do so again.

These are not hidden defects in the legislative process. These issues have been debated in Congress after Congress. I keep coming back to the central theme that public insistence, and public insistence alone, can remedy these difficulties through appropriate legislation. I have introduced such legislation, have myself conducted hearings on it, and as Chairman of the Committee on the Judiciary have appointed a Special Committee on Reapportionment. Thousands of copies of the hearings on the abolition of the Electoral College have been distributed to practically every high school and university in the land. Yet I have watched this legislation die in each Congress. It has never ceased to amaze me that legislation so patently necessary should take so many years of work, of oral and written argument, of hearings before subcommittees, of discussion in full committee, of debate on the floor, and going through a similar process in the other House, in Congress after Congress, only to begin the long road again with the next Congress.

In the matter of appropriation bills, for example, it would be relatively simple to prepare legislation which would permit the President to veto separate items and yet retain others which he felt to be necessary. An item veto would go a long way toward stopping pork barreling in Congress, reducing expenditures, and eliminating waste. Yet it has been virtually impossible to have such legislation enacted, despite the number of years it has been proposed.

It amazes me, for example, that the members of the House of Representatives submit to the tyranny of the Committee on Rules, composed of twelve members. When a bill is reported favorably by a full committee, the procedure is to ask the Committee on Rules to grant a rule for its consideration on the floor. Yet, the Rules Committee, with the exception of one Congress (the Eighty-first), has taken upon itself, through precedent, the consideration of each application for a rule as a mandate to reconsider the legislation on its merits. In many instances, the Committee on Rules has barred vital legislation from reaching the floor. In the Eighty-first Congress, after a bitter fight on the floor, the rules were amended so that the chairman of a committee could demand recognition by the Speaker for consideration of a bill if, after a certain period of time, the Committee on Rules had not acted thereon. In the Eighty-second Congress, in a fight equally bitter, this privilege of the chairman was withdrawn.

I do not share the views of many who exclaim that these are the most troubled times of our history, that war is inevitable and that the next war will erase the civilization we know, that ethics and morality are gone from government and gone from the people, and that we have no choice but to accept tyranny from the left or tyranny from the right. That these are parlous times no one can deny. But every age has had its challenge. While dynasties have tumbled and civilizations and cultures have been lost behind the curtain of centuries, the slow and, I for one say, inevitable march has gone forward to the realization of the individual's potential. In our gaze backward over these centuries, despite the nostalgic dreams of those seeking escape, we find how much misery, poverty, disease, and tyranny deprived the peoples of the world of life and living. It is the same whether you look to the twelfth or the sixteenth or the eighteenth or the nineteenth century, or go back to the dynasties before the Christian era. Slowly the lot of man has become better through the centuries. The heart and conscience of man have grown with each century. You cannot point to Hitlerism and Stalinism and say that this is not so. The march forward may be halted, but only for a while.

In one of his campaign speeches, Adlai Stevenson said, "There is nothing more important than people."

"That is it, exactly," I told myself when I heard the sentence. This is the truth toward which democracy gropes. This is what the Declaration of Independence said. It is the sum of the meaning of the Bill of Rights.

It is said glibly that the machine, particularly in the United States, has robbed the people of its soul; that the United States is materialistic; that the people of the United States are all cut to the same pattern with a deadly uniformity which has crushed the spirit and shrivelled imagination. It is incredible how many times the contrary has to be asserted, in view of all the evidence around us. In art, in literature, in science, in education, in productivity, and in government there is no country that matches the vigor, variety, the courage to break with the past when need be. The restless search is upon us.

It baffles me that this theme of the hollowness of the United States should find such credence, not only in certain circles in this country, but all through Europe. I consider it one of the major tasks of our foreign policy to explode this attitude. So keenly am I convinced of this that when I was invited to address the International Society of Italy (a quasi-governmental body) in

Rome, during the summer of 1951, I decided I would "speak my piece" on the subject. Guest as I was, I did not consider it a breach of taste or manners. I told them:

". . . In a most perverse and persistent manner, a —shall I say—fashionable portrait of the United States has shaped itself before the eyes of Europe and Asia. It is a portrait of a people brash, grasping, materialistic, alien to suffering, immature, self-absorbed and self-indulgent.

"No true understanding can be arrived at among the nations of the world until such impressions are corrected.

"Strangely enough, it is our unshakeable, basic belief in the idealism of man which has been most often misinterpreted. This basic belief, like a self-repeating motif, runs through our systems of jurisprudence, of education, of our political structure; in fact, throughout every relationship we have established, domestically and externally.

"It is not my purpose here today to glorify the United States, to defend it or extol it. I know only this: in the bitterness of our times, in the weight of words thrown about in mistrust and fear, the gap widens between nations and the bridge toward international understanding and collective security becomes harder to build.

"This caricature of the United States finds its way back to the people of the United States and the ghost of isolationism rears its head in hope again.

"I talk to you thus because in Italy, since World War II, a tremendous sensitivity of spirit inhabits your land, an articulate sensitivity to human needs, everywhere, to hungers of the mind, body and heart, everywhere. It is unmistakable. And nowhere, but nowhere, has the response been greater than in the United States.

"Our writers and artists have found in Italy that nourishment without which there is no creativity, and they, in turn, have brought this spirit back to us, to our everlasting enrichment. American writers—John Hersey, Alfred Hayes, Tennessee Williams, John Horne Burns—have found more than a facile fascination with the Italian scene. They have found the heart of Italy. Americans are reading Carlo Levi, Alberto Moravia, Elsa Morante, Riccardo Bacchelli, Giovanni Guareschi. The acknowledged artistry of Italian motion pictures, "Shoe Shine," "Open City," "Paisan," has helped effect that exchange of the coin of understanding. Suffice it to say that Americans and Italians are rediscovering each other, as a son of Italy once discovered America and America named its continent for another son of Italy."

274

If, after coming to Congress in 1922, I had left, let us say, after a period of some six years, I could not have written and spoken thus. The government was, shall I say, listless. Prohibition was the great national issue. I, myself, ran on a platform for the repeal of the Eighteenth Amendment. If the people were feverish about "flaming youth," they were limp about government. But we all awoke in a clanging and a clamor like the sounds in the night of hundreds of fire engines dashing to the flames. Now, as I look back and see how the inner discipline of a self-governing people met economic collapse, a world war, and face today a challenge as tense as any other they had faced before, it can be said that the democratic process is the strongest force that history has offered the people.

I am grateful that I have been privileged to watch and participate in a vital and perhaps revolutionary change in the concept of society's responsibilities to the people which compose it. I have seen the demand made on government to meet that change and answer it. In the TVA legislation, in the Social Security laws, in the move toward internationalism, in housing legislation, in old age benefits, in the protective legislation for banking and investments, in crop incentives, in slum clearance, there is a spelling out of the preciousness of the individual life. That this preciousness can be guarded without injury to the freedom of the people is the most stirring message of our democracy, the forerunner of a world yet to be.

I cannot thrust myself into the future. Swirling around in my mind are the questions of the atom bomb, the hydrogen bomb, Korea, the use of the veto power in the United Nations, the rearming of Germany, the hungry, distended bellies of children in Asia. Each question is related to the other, and there is no marking off where one begins and the other ends. Perhaps when we understand the relatedness of these problems, not only each to the other, but the relatedness to each of us, individually and personally, will the ragged pieces of the world fall in place. This will be the search. It will be mine, I know.

Index

278

Roosevelt, Franklin Delano, emotional response to, 19-20; on anti-trust laws, 140; on Jewish homeland in Israel, 117-118; on refugee welfare, 90-92; personality, 11-14; quarantine speech, 86, 238; Supreme Court reorganization, 14-19

Rules Committee tyranny, 270-271

Russell, Senator, 67

Sabath, Congressman, 81

St. Louis Post Dispatch, 174

San Francisco *Chronicle,* 188

Schram, Emil, 155

Securities Act, 20

Sexton, James J., 59-60

Sharett, Moshe, 133

Sherman Anti-Trust Law, 140, 161

Shorenstein, Hymie, 60-61, 62

Smith-Connally Act of 1943, 229-230

Smoot-Hawley Act, 8

State Government, 265-267

Steel industry inquiry, 156-161

Stein, Gunther, 173

Steinkraus, Herman, 155

Sternberg, Nachum, 134

Stevenson, Adlai, 72-76, 272

Stone, Dean, 46

Stratton, Congressman, 94

Supreme Court reorganization, 14-19

Taft-Hartley Act of 1947, 229, 230-231, 233

Television, 200, 264

Temple, Shirley, 187

Tennessee Valley Authority Act, 20

Thomas, Senator, 189

Time Magazine, 115, 174

Truman, Harry A., 23-24, 75, 118-119, 123, 148-152, 242

Un-American Activities Committee, 169-170, 183-194, 197-200

United Nations, 121, 240; future of, 244-256

United Nations Relief and Rehabilitation Administration, 89

United States Peace College, 235-238

United States Steel Company, 24, 156-160

Universal Military Training, 261-262

Venetian ironwork instructor, 43-44

Vishinsky, Andrei, 251

"Voice of Israel," 126

Volk, Dr. Lester, 60

Voorhis, Congressman, 208

Wagner Act, 222, 223, 226-229

Wallace, Henry A., 75

Walsh-Healey Act, 222

Walter, Congressman, 100

War Disputes Act of 1943, 229-230

War Refugee Board, 89

Washington Post, 174

Watson, Goodwin B., 186

Weisman, Celler, Quinn, Allan and Spett, 59

Weizmann, Chaim, 133

Williams, Tennessee, 274

Willkie, Wendell, 239

Wilson, Charles E., 155

Wine salesman, 34-49

World War II, 3, 240

Zionism, 113-123